G000126645

TALES FROM THE
CITY

TALES FROM THE
CITY

A collection of writing inspired
by Norwich City Football Club

Volume One
Edited by Mick Dennis

TALES FROM
www.talesfrom.com

First published in Great Britain in 2015
by Tales From

Printed and bound by SS Media

ISBN 978-0-993-2381-1-6

Tales From Ltd
2 Gaddesden Lane, Redbourn, St Albans, AL3 7NP
Registered company number: 9082738

www.talesfrom.com
info@talesfrom.com

TALES FROM THE CITY

CONTENTS

INTRODUCTION

BY THE EDITOR

Welcome to this collection of 'Tales' about Norwich City, each written by either a former player or a supporter. These are pieces of original writing, and every one is distinctly different.

And to be frank, some differ profoundly from what I had expected. All I set out to do, after accepting the invitation to commission and edit an anthology of essays about the club, was to produce a book I would enjoy reading.

Bryan Gunn, City's goalkeeper for the most successful spell in the club's history, had to be included. But he wanted to tell a difficult Tale: how and why, after many different roles at Carrow Road, he became manager – and how that final job ended with the sack. It's a searingly honest account, with no happy ending.

Of course I wanted Iwan Roberts and Grant Holt. They are two of the greatest strikers to have pulled on yellow shirts. They embodied the hopes and aspirations of City fans and never let us down. They didn't disappoint with their contributions for this book, either. But they did surprise me.

I wasn't expecting Iwan to recall how difficult it was for him when he first arrived in Norfolk. I was not prepared for Holty to detail how he nearly didn't sign. They explain in their Tales that, not only did they both thrive eventually, but, for some unknown reason, both particularly relished beating a team from Suffolk.

Holty talks about a certain hat-trick. Iwan recounts being told not to celebrate too loudly in the changing room after scoring both goals in a 2-0 win at Portman Road. He ignored the instruction.

The other ex-footballer I wanted was Paul McVeigh. I've shared a radio studio with him, and had a couple of nights out. So I knew he could tell a good Tale. And I knew that behind the readiness to enjoy the dawn delights of Prince Of Wales Road is someone who thinks deeply about the game and about life. Again, his essay surprised; he really struggled at Norwich after being released by Spurs.

When it came to thinking of fans to produce Tales about City, my wish-list started with a couple of 'proper' writers.

Lilie Ferrari, a novelist and scriptwriter, lives and slaves away at her computer in Norwich. She seldom misses a Carrow Road game and, having fairly frequently sat next to her, I can report she is a very sore loser. She was the first person I approached.

Getting Michael Wynn Jones to contribute was a coup, I believe. His voice is seldom heard, because he understands that the media might choose to talk to his wife, who just happens to be Delia Smith. But I have had the absolute delight of sharing many hours talking about Norwich City with him over the last 15 years or so, and now you can read his brilliant description of how a chap who used to stand at the River End found himself in the boardroom and at the very kernel of some great dramas.

Securing the 'voice' of one of the club's joint owners, led me to realise that I needed the man who is the voice of Norwich City for thousands. Chris Goreham is the fan with the BBC Radio Norfolk microphone.

I wanted Jon Rogers because I think he's a genius. He is a singer, song-writer, poet, humourist and columnist. He uses the pseudonym BigGrantHolt on YouTube and Twitter. Oh, and he included a picture of my family and me in the video for *At*

The Game, his moving song about the Wembley play-off final.

Sticking with people I admire, I bagged Charlie Wyett, of *The Sun*, and Simon Thomas from *Sky Sports*. Both are City nutters. I worked for the *Sun* in the 'old days' of Fleet Street. The pressure to get belting stories every day made it the most stressful time of my career. So hats off to Hunstanton-born Charlie, who has remained fairly sane despite doing the job for 17 years.

I've done bits and pieces of live 'telly' too, and it takes a sharp mind and an unflappable nature to excel at that particular medium. And, as Simon explains in his Tale, being a City fan can, on occasions, add to the pressure.

Finally, I wanted to write my own Tale – about why I owe so much to one Norwich manager. So that gave me 11 writers: the right number, surely, for a football book.

As the chapters began arriving, so some common themes emerged. Simon Thomas and Chris Goreham both pay tribute to the late Roy Waller, a giant of local broadcasting. Simon and Michael Wynn Jones were introduced to Norwich City by their clergymen fathers. Jon Rogers's dad was his companion at all his formative City experiences. Charlie Wyett takes his son to matches…

But the real common denominator is passionate affection for Norwich City. It survives in Bryan Gunn. It flourishes still in Iwan Roberts, Grant Holt and Paul McVeigh. It is what compelled Michael Wynn Jones to help save the club. It is what all of us who have written our Tales have in common.

So I hope you like love stories. Here are 11 of them.

Mick Dennis

1

After a magnificent playing career, **Bryan Gunn** continued to serve Norwich City, doing whatever was asked of him.

Finally, he stepped forward and stepped up when the club was without a manager.

Here, for the first time, he talks about what happened next. He discloses new details of that era and reveals how the crushing despair of relegation ended an ambition that has remained a secret until now.

This is his honest, highly personal account of how his 22 years at Carrow Road ended.

KEEPING WES, SIGNING HOLTY...
AND LOSING MY JOB

BY BRYAN GUNN

This is the final chapter. I don't know where it will be in the book, but it's my last chapter. I've told the story of my goalkeeping career, and of growing up on a farm in Thurso and so on, in my autobiography, *In Where It Hurts*, which I wrote with Kevin Piper very nearly a decade ago. So this has to be about what happened next: about when, in one sense, I hurt the most.

But, for those who don't know, I played 477 games for Norwich City FC and they included some very successful seasons for the club. Then, in February 1998, I moved to Hibernian but only lasted a year because I broke my leg.

I actually applied for the job of managing Norwich when Mike Walker left the second time. I also applied to be Colchester manager. I applied by fax both times – younger readers will have to ask someone what a fax is! The reply from Colchester chairman Peter Heard said, 'Thank you for your application, but please note how my name is spelled.' I'd got it wrong. But Mel Henderson, an Ipswich-based journalist who had encouraged me to make the application, was the one who had told me how the chairman's name was spelled and he had got it wrong. Never trust a journalist!

Then Norwich chief executive Gordon Bennett and Andy Cullen, who was the director of sales and marketing, offered me the chance to go back to Carrow Road and work in the commercial department, which they had set out to revitalise.

So, from 1999 to 2007 I had a variety of roles within the club, all of which I really enjoyed and all of which were worthwhile.

But when Peter Grant became manager at the start of 2007 he wanted me to be part of his backroom team. He wanted someone who knew all about the club to be in the offices at the training ground to deal with scouts, agents, players and so on when he was out on the pitch taking training. That got me into the football department.

While I was working under Granty I explained that I wanted to resume my coaching qualifications courses. I'd got my B licence and started my A licence as a 23-year-old in Aberdeen and thought now would be an opportunity to get studying again. Granty okayed it for me to go to Warwick University for a refresher course for the B licence and he also agreed that I should do some coaching with the kids to get the hours on the training pitch that the licence required.

But then Granty lost his job. The results weren't good and after a particularly awful performance at QPR, when Norwich became the first team to lose there that season, Granty resigned. Glenn Roeder got the job, and he did not want me involved in the coaching at first. I knocked on his door at the training ground and said, 'I've been working as the club liaison and doing some coaching hours for my B licence.' He told me to forget about the coaching because he wanted me to concentrate on the liaison. He had his own coaching guys, as many managers do.

But he was happy for me to do recruitment. One of the first things he did was get rid of chief scout Alan Wood, who had worked for Mike Walker at Everton and had then come to Carrow Road when Mike returned for his second spell. Glenn was having a shake-up of coaching and scouting and I began basically running the scouting department from the training ground.

It was an important role; a proper involvement. It meant that I was part of Glenn's inner circle and, eventually, he asked me to work as goalkeeping coach, on top of my other duties, for six months. That meant I was coaching David Marshall and Matt Gilks. Joe Lewis was out on loan to Peterborough, but Declan Rudd and Jedd Steer were coming through from the youth system and I even coached my son, Angus, during the school holidays.

I was very much involved in the football side, and it went well, because we stayed up, which had been very much in doubt at one time. We were bottom when Glenn came in.

The last game of the season was at Sheffield Wednesday, and we were safe by the time we played that game. Dion Dublin had announced that he was retiring, and got a massive send-off from the travelling Norwich fans, but Darren Huckerby got nothing like the same amount of cheering and chanting. Those of us inside the club knew that Hucks was finishing as a Norwich player too that day, but it hadn't been announced and, in theory, there was still a possibility that he would be offered a new contract – but that wasn't a real likelihood, because there was quite a personality clash between Hucks and Glenn. I thought it was a shame that the crowd didn't know that it was time to say farewell to Hucks and didn't really chant his name or anything.

That summer, while I was head of recruitment, Glenn's signings included Wes Hoolahan and Sammy Clingan. We brought in two centre-backs, John Kennedy on loan from Celtic and Dejan Stefanovic from Fulham for a million. We thought we had the makings of a decent team, but we looked a bit short of goals. In an attempt to solve that, on the last day of the summer transfer window Glenn signed Antoine Sibierski, who had played for him at Newcastle, on loan from Wigan.

Both the centre-backs got crocked. Kennedy suffered bad

ankle ligament damage and then an old knee injury flared up as well. He returned to Celtic. Stefanovic ruptured his cruciate knee ligaments after 12 games and never kicked a ball for us again. But it was the Sibierski deal that really hurt us. He only scored twice in 16 games and then got injured. I don't know if we had to pay all his wages or half of them, but he was on £25,000 a week at Wigan, so signing him and then not being able to use him made a big dent in our budget for not much return.

Meanwhile, I was scouting players in the lower divisions. In November 2008, the first team had a Saturday evening game at Nottingham Forest, which we won 2-1. On the afternoon before that game I went along to Lincoln to see them play Shrewsbury. That game ended 0-0, but I got my first sight of a decent striker who was playing for Shrewsbury. His strike partner, Richard Walker, was sent off very early on for a late challenge on the goalkeeper, and so the other guy had to play up front on his own. He looked a bit of a lump, but whenever a ball came forward, none of the defenders got a touch. He knocked them about, won the header, controlled the ball and brought someone else into play. I marked down his name: Grant Holt.

The win at Forest that day was only the fifth of the season, and we had played 19 games. That sort of form – occasional wins spread thinly among some really bad results – continued. In January we lost a Tuesday night home FA Cup replay against Charlton 1-0. The fans were understandably in a black mood and there were demonstrations against Glenn. The next day, at Colney, I was there when it all ended for him.

Chairman Roger Munby and chief executive Neil Doncaster went into Glenn's room and came out a while later. My office was over the way from the manager's office, so they came and stood in my office to keep out of the way, but Glenn came over and shook my hand to say goodbye.

When that happens at a football club it's horrible: like a funeral. The run of results and performances created the situation, but it meant that others went as well. Lee Clark had left two months earlier to become Huddersfield manager, but when Glenn was sacked Paul Stephenson went and so too did Adam Sadler – no, not the actor – who had only joined about a week earlier to oversee the reserves.

When the chairman and chief exec were still at Colney I said, 'If you want someone to take the team at the weekend, I'll do it, if it will help the club.' They did a second take but I said, 'Yes, I'll do it. Ricky Martin [the academy manager and youth team coach] and Tommy Wright [goalkeeping coach] can take the training sessions and I'll do everything else.'

I didn't even think about it really before making that offer. It was something that needed to be done, and so I offered. It was the least I could do after what the club had meant to me over the years. In my mind at that stage, I assumed it would be a short-term thing, but I wanted to do it to the best of my ability.

So we made sure the preparation for the next game went well. Glenn's sacking was on the Wednesday. That meant we had two days to prepare for the Saturday match at home to Barnsley. We needed to change the mood and lift spirits and we did that. Then I had to decide upon a team and that meant leaving some people out. I had never been in that situation before as manager, but I'd been involved in enough matches to know what it was like for players, and so I wanted to talk individually to those I was leaving out, rather than just read out the team list.

I made sure Wes Hoolahan was in the team. I felt he was a special player. He could be infuriating to managers, but if you got him playing and enjoying himself, you could be in business. I knew Darel Russell didn't like being striker but I needed him there. So I sat him down and explained, 'Rusty I'll try and get you back into midfield as soon as possible, but I need you to do a job in attack'. And I phoned Sir Alex Ferguson, who had been my manager at Aberdeen, and asked him for pointers for the team talk. He said, 'Keep it simple.'

Susan and I had arranged a weekend away: not far, but we lived in Framingham Pigot, four miles outside the city, and we were due to go with pals to a hotel in north Norfolk to celebrate a good friend's 50th birthday. We were due to be there for two nights, Friday and Saturday; I hadn't been expecting to be managing a team in an important Championship match! I couldn't let people down, so Susan and I still went up on the Friday night but, of course, I was thinking only about the game. I stuck to sparkling water and I might have had a glass of diluted white wine.

When the time came to drive to the stadium the next day, I was ready. And, walking from the car, all the fans were wishing me well – 'Good luck Gunny!' – and the atmosphere was really positive, which was a big, big change from the demonstrations four days earlier.

I did have a special rapport with Norwich fans. It began in my playing days, and I think some of it was due to what had happened with our daughter Francesca. We found out she had leukaemia at the end of a season, in the May. I had been away for a week on an end of season club trip, and came back to learn that news. Susan had taken her to hospital that day and the specialist actually came around to our house to tell us the prognosis. From the next day we were at a hospital in Cambridge and we spent all summer in hospitals: the regional centre at Cambridge or the Norfolk and Norwich every time there was an infection or anything.

We didn't say anything about the situation publicly, but when all her hair fell out because of the chemo, I shaved my head completely so that she was like her daddy. Eventually, I had to explain why I had suddenly made myself bald and so the fans knew what was going on in our family. Of course, the supporters were magnificent. I am not going to dwell on Francesca's death in this chapter, because this piece is about a different era and because I dealt with it fully in the book I wrote with Kevin Piper – but I do believe that the whole stadium was with me when I took to the pitch to keep goal a few days after our little girl passed away, and I think the Norwich fans stayed with me till the moment the final whistle went on my playing career at the club, and beyond. We had a connection.

I think as well, though, that goalkeepers often have a special relationship with fans, partly because of the proximity and partly because it is such an individual role in a team-game. And down the years Norwich have had special men in the role. Kevin Keelan was the one I got to know a little. Before him was Sandy Kennon, who sadly died while this book was being prepared. And I followed Chris Woods.

At the time I arrived, Jimmy Greaves was making jokes every weekend on TV about Scottish goalkeepers, but after a few dodgy games, I did okay for Norwich. We finished fifth in my first season, then fourth and two seasons later we were third in the Premier League. Fergie had told me I was a top six goalkeeper and said that, although I was going to Norwich, I should set my sights higher. I didn't. I stayed at Norwich and helped them become a top six club.

Anyway, all those years later, I was manager and when I came out onto the pitch to give the crowd a wave before that first game, there was a terrific reception for me. But there was a job to be done. And boy, did they do it well. They won 4-0. I had paid special attention to Wes and Rusty in the build-up, so I was delighted that they played huge parts in the victory. Wes got the first goal and Rusty the last, but they did a lot more than score.

After the game, I was aware that there were conversations going on here and there involving the chairman, but I wasn't worried about that because we'd done what we'd set out to do: steady the ship, change the mood and post a good performance and a great result.

At the press conference, one of the journalists asked, 'Are you aware that the club are holding interviews on Monday for the new manager?' Of course, I wasn't so I told them. I said I was just going to relax, attend a birthday party and see what happens. And that's what I did. Lots of the people at the party in north Norfolk had been to the game to support me, and it turned into a hell of a party! There was even a huge food fight. Of course I caught everything thrown at me.

At seven the next morning, I was woken by a call from Dion Dublin. 'Gunny, you've got to go for it. I talked to some of the lads last night and they are for you. You've got to go for it – and I'll come with you. I'll be your number two.'

Susan was still sleeping but Dion had got me thinking. When she woke up I told her about the call and that I was considering putting my hat into the ring. After breakfast we all went for a walk along Holkham beach and after a while I said, 'Susan, I've got to go for it.'

But I knew I'd got to put together a coaching team – a dream team – before I talked to the club. All the other candidates would turn up with laptop presentations and speeches, but I'd never done this before so I knew I needed to pull a rabbit out of the hat. My 'rabbit' would be a clutch of coaches with a special feel for Norwich City.

I thought straight away of Ian Crook, who was working in Australia, which is where he had finished his career. I knew he had admirers on the board. I got hold of his number and rang him. He was ready to jump on a plane already, so someone had already suggested it to him. So I had Dion and Crooky.

Next I thought of John Deehan, who had been a player, coach and then manager at Norwich. I knew he wasn't doing much by then, but I also knew he was a great football man. So if I could have him as chief scout, it would also give me a wise head to talk things through with. He would be a good mentor as well as being a good chief scout.

Ian Butterworth was another who would be perfect. He was Hartlepool manager, which would make him more difficult to get to Norwich, but it would be worth the effort.

So, that same day, the Sunday, I phoned Neil Doncaster and said, 'I believe you are holding interviews tomorrow'. I was able to tell him the hotel they were using for the interviews, so he could see I meant business. I said, 'I want to be on your list.' He phoned me back a few minutes later after talking to Delia and Michael I imagine. Yep, I would be the last person they saw the following afternoon.

But then Dion came back to me and said that he didn't think he would be able to get out of his contract with Sky Sports, which was a blow. But when the interview went ahead I was full of passion, still stoked by the response from the players and the crowd. The interview went well.

At 11 that night, I got a call saying, 'Come to Carrow Road.' When I got there, Mr Doncaster was on the phone trying to secure Ian Butterworth to work alongside me. But I was fully aware that someone else might be on a different line some-where else in the offices talking to one or more of the other candidates for the top job. I understand that Paul Ince, Ian Holloway and Iain Dowie were interviewed.

But about half an hour after I had walked in, things fell into place for the board. They knew they hadn't got Dion, but they had sorted out Butterworth and knew they could get Crook. They had John Deehan. And they had me.

When I left the job a few short months later, some people said that I had been a poor appointment because I was completely inexperienced. But I had wanted to be a manager or coach since I was 23 when I had started taking my coaching badges, and I had always tried to learn as I went along in my career. At Aberdeen, I'd gone to matches in the evenings, travelling with Fergie. Him and Archie Knox, his right-hand man, used to go to games – anywhere a ball moved – and I went on quite a few of those trips, listening to them in the car and learning. All the time I was playing I used to watch what other teams did in their warm-ups, for instance, and how different managers changed things during games. Then I did all that scouting and co-ordinating other scouts, so that I got detailed analyses of tactics and so on. Also, I had played for some very good managers. And when my turn came to be a manager, I had a really good team of coaches. On the internet, people said we didn't know what we were doing, but that could not be further from the truth. We were all experienced football people who all knew exactly what we were trying to do.

Paul Lambert, who replaced me, used to say, even when things were going really well, that he was always only three bad games away from the sack. Well, I think that during my time as Norwich manager, we were only a few results away from being a success. In total, my Norwich record was six wins, five draws and ten defeats. But six of the defeats were by a single goal and if just three of them had gone slightly differently... All right, 'if' is a very big word in football, but honestly, we weren't far away.

When we went to QPR on a filthy wet Tuesday night in March, showed grit and determination, had magnificent support and won 1-0, I felt we could do it. I thought that night that the lads were up for it and we would be all right. Rusty scored about 20 minutes from the end and, with our fans roaring their support, we dug in and held on.

We were playing at Blackpool the following Saturday and the players said they wanted to fly up to have the best possible preparation and that they would pay for their own tickets. That showed their intent. So I went to the board and they agreed to pay towards the flights, but the players did cough up some of their own cash too. We turned up, it was a terrible pitch, Charlie Adams scored one of his special goals and we ended up losing 2-0, which knocked us right back after the QPR performance. That was a killer.

Physically and mentally I stayed strong and didn't let the pressure affect me. I worked as hard as was possible to improve a situation that was not exactly wonderful when I took over. And I thought, to the very last moment, that we were in with a chance. Even going to Charlton on the last day, I thought we could do it. One of the factors was that I knew we would have absolutely massive support behind us. And so, in the dressing room before the game, I told them, 'Don't get your names in the history of Norwich City FC for the wrong reason. Let's get the result here, and then turn the page.'

When it was still at 0-0, we learned that Plymouth were winning at Barnsley, which meant that, at that moment, we were out of the relegation spots. The Norwich fans packed behind the goal away to my right went absolutely wild. Yet that moment seemed to make the players more tense. They went into hiding and it was one, two, three... the goals flew in.

At the finish we had lost 4-2 and were relegated to the third tier. I was shell-shocked; the emptiest I have ever felt in a sporting or professional context. I'd had a very similar feeling as a player when we were relegated from the Premier League in 1995 in the last game of the season at Leeds, but that day at Charlton was even worse. The directors went on the field to sort of face the fans and to thank them for their support and I had tears in my eyes when I saw Delia and Michael doing that.

I told them how sorry I was. It was hard. So were the press interviews afterwards.

It was a horrible coach journey back. The lads who lived in the south stayed and didn't come back with us, and I don't think I said goodbye to them at all because I was numb.

The next day I learned that there were to be meetings at the club all day as Delia and Michael came to grips with what had happened and decided what to do. Towards me there was an acknowledgement of some of the work I had done and an understanding that I had been striving all the time.

What they didn't know – what nobody but Susan knew – was that relegation changed my mind about my own position. If we had stayed up, I would have stepped aside and sought a role as director of football. I would have told the board that I thought the club needed a restructure – which is what I did think – and that they should decide whether Ian Butterworth, Ian Crook or someone else entirely should be manager, but that I would like to take a new position.

Ultimately, as manager, you have to make the club your number one priority. It is a job that requires total commitment. You can't have any time off. You are taking and making phone calls: to your chief exec, to agents, to players. And when you are not actually doing anything, you are thinking about doing something for the club, for the team. It is constant. That's why mangers get paid good wages. And for every minute of every week when I was Norwich City manager, I gave the job everything I had to give. But from about six games from the end of that first season I thought that once we had stayed up I would try for a job at the club that would allow me to give my family a bit more of my time.

As it was though, we had been relegated and there could be no question of me quitting if the club wanted me to try and right that wrong. Relegation was a failure and I felt I couldn't quit then. I felt I had to do everything I could to put things right, if I was given the chance.

And I was. They told me to carry on. I believe their thought process was that I had stepped up when they needed someone and now I should be given a chance to assemble my own team, have a full pre-season and a proper go at it.

I talked to the players and asked them who was up for the challenge. Wes was one that I knew would be wanted by other clubs, but one that I needed to keep at Norwich City. He wanted to play at the highest level possible, but I sat down with him and had a big conversation with him. I said that if he stayed but things did not go well, I would guarantee he could leave in the January. That was what I had to say in the circumstances we were in.

Lee Croft was another I tried hard to persuade to stay. But he left for Derby and twice what we could pay. David Marshall left for Cardiff, Sammy Clingan went to Coventry. It was quite an exodus.

But I signed 12 players that summer, trying to bring in value and as much quality as I could afford but also players who would be prepared to scrap their way out of League One and bond together as a unit. Matt Gill was the first. The Grant Holt deal went through, thanks to the generosity of director Michael Foulger and the fans. Chris Martin and Mickey Spillane had been outcasts under Glenn, but they were back from a loan at Luton and I told them they would have a fair chance with me. And I signed a goalkeeper, Michael Theoklitos. He was Australian but despite what people assumed later, he wasn't just some bloke who came straight from the beach. He had been Australia's top keeper and had been over in England the season before, training at Blackpool and then at Everton and then with us. I spoke to Chris Woods at Everton about him and we had him training with us in the season before the summer in which he signed for us. We also signed Ben Alnwick, a good young keeper on loan from Spurs, so it wasn't as if I was putting all my goalkeeping eggs in one basket for League One – which was just as well, because with the sort of day he had on his debut, Michael would have dropped them all.

We were not the best payers in League One, but we offered competitive wages with a good bonus structure, incentivised to get success, and we could promise players that they would be playing in front of a full house every week at Carrow Road because, fantastically, the fans had stayed incredibly loyal and all the season tickets had been sold.

Jens Berthel Askou, the Danish defender who could head the ball further than most could kick it, joined us while we were on a pre-season mini tour of Scotland, based at the University of St Andrews, and the whole pre-season went well. It certainly wasn't a holiday camp. The players were worked hard and everything looked good.

We knew that with so many new players the team would have to settle and evolve over the course of the season, but we thought we were in good shape for the first game of the campaign, at home to Colchester. We did start well. For the first ten minutes we were like Real Madrid. But after that we were real shite.

Michael had a poor game, but so did most of the others. We were 4-0 down after 20 minutes and 5-0 down at half-time. I ripped into them. But when I asked them what on earth had happened out there, Wes said, 'We're tired'. I couldn't believe it. Tired? After 45 minutes of the first game of season? I picked up Gary Doherty's suntan cream and threw the bottle so hard that it smashed against the wall. The cream went over people's suits. I told them to win the second half. But they couldn't. They lost the half 2-1 and the game 7-1.

I told them they had to be at Colney the next day, and on

that Sunday I made them sit and watch the game again in the TV room. I told them they had ruined my Sunday so I was ruining theirs – but I wanted them to look at things in the game and realise they could and must do a lot better.

We travelled down to Exeter on the Monday, trained at Exeter University and played at Yeovil in the League Cup on the Tuesday night. I dropped the goalkeeper, Holty scored three and we won 4-0. There was a really big away contingent, which was typical for Norwich. They'd just seen their team thrashed 7-1 and it was only a cup game at the other end of the country, but they still turned up. I am glad I gave them something to cheer about that day because it was my last game as manager.

We stayed down because we were playing at Exeter on the Saturday. I got a call on the Friday that David McNally was coming down to see me. While I waited for him I came to the conclusion that he was coming to tell me I was out of a job. And I was right.

So I made my way back by train from Exeter on my own, leaving the players behind and leaving my career at a club which had been a major part of my life. In total, I had spent 22 years at Carrow Road in just about every possible role. But it was over. That night I reached Norwich station after three trains, about six hours, dozens of calls from friends and more than one bottle of wine.

That's a long time ago now and the world has moved on, the club has moved on, and so have I, with a new life and new career in the north-west.

I am still proud of the team I left behind that day– with Wes, Holty, Chrissy Martin and the rest – and I don't think any of them have said anything derogatory about me. I am certainly not bitter. I can't spend my life being bitter. So when Norwich won the play-off final at Wembley against Middlesbrough, I texted Delia and Michael Wynn Jones to congratulate them.

When I meet David McNally, we always shake hands.

My sadness is that there must be a generation of fans who only know me as the manager who lost 7-1 against Colchester. My own memories of Norwich City are different. They include those 477 games, three top five finishes in the top division, and several rewarding roles after I finished playing. My memories also include that special rapport I had with the fans when I was playing. I had no hair but they didn't care!

Bryan Gunn was City's player of the year twice and the keeper of our dreams. Then he worked for the club in a variety of roles until, after 22 years as an NCFC man, he stepped forward to become manager.

2

He used to stand on the terraces. Then
came the time he needed to stand by
the club. After four decades as a fan,
Michael Wynn Jones and his wife,
Delia Smith, stepped in to save
Norwich City.

Now, another two decades on, here is
a unique perspective from the fan who
became an owner.

He takes us back with him to the
games which made him fall in love
with the club, to the Thai meal at
which a huge loan was agreed and into
the boardroom for the insider's
perspective of football and financial
dramas, turmoil and triumphs.

RECOLLECTIONS FROM THE RIVER END
AND ELSEWHERE

BY MICHAEL WYNN JONES

I would say it's been a game of two unequal halves, the first spanning some 40 years or so, the second a mere 20 so far. In Norfolk it's no big deal, but I have been going to Carrow Road for more than 60 years, years that have spanned playing Newport County in the Third Division South to playing Inter Milan in Europe, that have witnessed the surrender of open terraces to corporate hospitality, and the escalation of players' wages by 10,000 per cent. It's progress of a sort, I suppose, but part of me is still nostalgic for those uncomplicated, less commercial days that helped to fashion my footballing passion.

THE FIRST HALF

I went to my first football match with my father in Aldershot where he was vicar and whose parish encompassed the football ground (The Rec, where the best view was on the hill behind the turnstiles which in desperation they would open at half-time and let you in for free). He became a Norfolk vicar a few years later, a football-mad Norfolk vicar. Just how football-mad he was my mother had discovered (if she didn't already know) when the big treat of her honeymoon in London was a ticket for the Boxing Day match between Charlton Athletic and Chelsea. It is true parishioners had an annoying habit of getting married at three on a Saturday afternoon, but it didn't inconvenience him too much in Norfolk as at that time he had care of only 250 souls most of whom were already married.

So it was that, on a freezing cold day in April 1955, we battled our way for the first time along the riverside and up the mound that was then the River End, and squeezed ourselves into the heaving mass. 'Look on the bright side,' said my father. 'We won't have to worry about Charlie Billington here.' Charlie Billington was the then Aldershot defender, whose turning circle had been compared to that of a World War One battleship. Except he wasn't any more! He was the Canaries' latest signing and had made his way to Norfolk at exactly the same time as us.

Charlie lasted till the following season, as I recall, at which point Norwich (teetering on the brink of bankruptcy) had to apply for re-election to the Football League. It was very ungentlemanly to vote anyone out of the league in those days, so the Canaries survived to celebrate three years later what was, certainly at that point, their greatest moment – 'The 1959 Cup Run' (forever celebrated with capital letters and inverted commas). My own memories of it are, at best, eclectic: the snow-covered pitch with only the white lines cleared, on which we, and Terry Bly in particular, dispatched Man U with ease; the legend of Ken Nethercott who played the last half-hour against Sheffield United with one arm hanging uselessly at his side after dislocating his shoulder; and the excitement of that opening goal at White Hart Lane from Terry Allcock, who was burying defenders long before he became a funeral director.

Above all, though, I still picture the sea of rosettes and cacophony of rattles – and that was just all over the city in the days leading up to a match. Mind you, so tightly packed in were we at Carrow Road, all 38,000 of us, that no-one could hope to wield a rattle, that curious instrument that had originally been issued during the war (so my father confided to me) to warn of gas attacks by the Germans. There was no scope for movement of any kind in those crowds; even those who had brought their own plastic bottles to cope with the consequence of six pre-match pints were paralysed. Nevertheless the crowds had a kind of internal momentum, usually a collective surge forward as a dangerous attack on goal developed. You very quickly learnt to find a spot in front of the crush barrier.

Certain rituals were as ingrained into the fabric of a match-day as the wafting aromas of fried onions over the River End that signalled there was a maximum of five more minutes to play. There was the regal progress around the ground of Captain Canary, decked out in those days with top hat, waist-coat, white gloves and a cigar, a somewhat ambivalent contrast to the terraces where flat caps were still *de rigueur* (though the odd bobble-hat here and there gave hints of what was to come).

Whatever activity there may or may not have been on the field before the interval, at half-time the pitch buzzed with energy. On came the corps of forkers and stampers attending to the furrows that invariably appeared on the pitch in those days. True there were no substitutes warming up because none were permitted, but the touchline swarmed with capped gents touring with the lucky lottery number chalked up on a black-board, with others straining on a huge blanket to catch any donations for the charity of the day, and yet others with trays of chocolates and sweets which they would hurl into the crowd if the correct change had been hurled at them first.

But the main action came with the arrival of the Drayton Silver Marching Band, who would make stately advances up and down the pitch, with their medley of popular marches. They always contrived to be at the far end of the pitch when the referee and players returned for the second half, but reso-lutely refused to change step as they made for the exit, dodging the balls being lobbed about by the teams and thus ensuring their ovation as they finally disappeared through the gate. For a short while it was the Dagenham Girl Pipers strutting their stuff round the pitch, I recall, with a massive 'whoosh!' echoing round the ground each time the majorette twirled her mace high into the air, followed by a collective wolf-whistle as she caught it safely above her head.

City's stuttering progress through the Second Division during the Sixties culminated in Ron Saunders' team gaining promotion to the First in 1972, followed shortly afterwards by the agony of our first visit to Wembley for the League Cup final. Losing 1-0 to Spurs was bad enough, but the message on the illuminated scoreboard at the end – forever lasered onto my brain – offered no consolation. It read, 'Hard Luck Norwich. You Put Up A Brave Fight'. What I wanted it to say was, 'If That Last-Minute Lunge By Big Dunc Had Not Missed By Two Inches It Would Have Been A Very Different Story!'

Two years later another League Cup final and another 1-0 defeat, this time to Aston Villa, a scoreline that undoubtedly saved Delia considerable indignity. Somehow or other she found herself at Wembley sitting in the middle of the Aston Villa supporters, somewhat conspicuous by her large yellow-and-green rosette. During the game she might as well have been an alien from outer space for all the communication there was, but at the final whistle her neighbours launched a charm offensive, 'Hard luck, luv!' They might have patted her on the head, but at least they didn't say we had put up a brave fight.

As we moved into the era of £1,000-a-week footballers (though none of them at Norwich one suspects) so were they assuming the mantle of leaders of fashion. Players in the Seventies and Eighties scarcely matched the exotic coiffures, braids and dreadlocked hair of the modern game, but they certainly had more of it. The shining exception (literally) was Bill Punton, whose glistening pate streaking down the wing for Norwich was a sight to wonder at. On the other hand Kevin

Keelan's immaculately manicured mop never seemed to have a strand out of place – except when the goalpost at Wolves fell on top of him and he was carried off. Trevor Hockey epitomized the 'Neanderthal' look, which permitted only space for the eyes and reflected his primeval approach to football. Then there was Graham Paddon: while football shorts got shorter and tighter, Graham's golden locks got longer and looser. Defenders would have grabbed it by the handful if they could have got anywhere near him.

Then began the yo-yo years, in spite of the fact that John Bond and Ken Brown notched up 14 consistent years in the manager's seat between them. After the glory days of 1972 and our first promotion to the top division, there followed a spate of relegations (1974, 1980, 1985). But in each case the Canaries bounced back magnificently at the first attempt, leading to a mindset among us supporters that if it ever happened again we only had to turn up to regain our rightful place. Of course, it did happen again, in 1995, and whoever printed those posters at the beginning of the next season, 'On Loan To The Endsleigh League', found they had tempted fate once too often.

To celebrate our ascension to the First Division in 1972, we decided season tickets in the City Stand were necessary. It was a whole new way of life. For a start there was free coffee or Bovril at half-time – rumour had it there were biscuits as well but we never got out in time to find out. Hand-written team sheets were pinned up on a board before the match for our approval or otherwise. There were cushions too, for an extra 10p, until they were withdrawn because too often they finished up in the vicinity of linesmen who had incurred someone's displeasure. Above all it was a different perspective on the game: within spitting distance of the dugout, we felt we could engage in the proceedings much more intimately.

Then one morning in October 1984 we woke up to learn it had all gone up in smoke, quite literally. In the early hours an electrical fault (reportedly) sparked a major conflagration in the City stand. The antiquated wooden structure didn't stand a chance and our seats were cinders, along with the boardroom, changing rooms and trophy cabinet. We were relocated to the upper tier of the recently completed River End stand, just above one of those new-fangled executive boxes. It was from this vantage point that we witnessed one of the most celebrated goals in the Canary canon: Stevie Bruce's thundering header at the death to knock Ipswich out of the semi-final of the League Cup.

Which took us to Wembley yet again, for the Friendly Final against Sunderland, whom we had cunningly confused by letting them beat us the week before in the league. As it was, Asa Hartford's deflected goal and Clive Walker's heart-stopping penalty miss ensured us our first major trophy. In truth I don't recall how much camaraderie there was on the pitch but certainly both sets of fans stood out as beacons of decency in an era of hooliganism, engaging in impromptu kick-abouts on Wembley Way before the game. The other unifying factor, I suppose, was both of us getting relegated at the end of the season!

Does anyone remember the Super Cup, probably the most ill-fated competition of all time? It was devised to financially compensate those clubs who were barred from Europe in the aftermath of the Heysel tragedy: no-one would televise it, hardly anyone watched it, it only survived one year and even then the final had to be postponed till the next season. Norwich qualified by virtue of their Wembley triumph, but the only significant fact that I can recall is that we drew twice with mighty Man U and put them out of the competition (and saw the beginning of my growing conviction of Norwich's invincibility against the Reds at Carrow Road – which lasted for at least the next five years).

Once we were back in a spanking new City Stand we watched the plucky Canaries more than hold their own back in the top flight – indeed finishing high enough in two seasons to be robbed yet again of a European adventure. Then in 1992-93 came the *annus mirabilis* when the club topped the Premier League from the end of August to the middle of March. Somewhere in one of the lobbies of the City Stand there used to be an engraved plaque of the league table on March 24 1993, the first line of which read:

1. Norwich City P36 W19 D8 L9 Pts 65

I rarely failed to stop and look at it when I passed although I knew it by heart. But for one gut-wrenching week at the beginning of April, when Man U finally beat us at home on the Monday (so much for my invincibility theory) and we shipped in five goals against Spurs on the Friday, we could have made it all the way. Couldn't we?

As it was we made it to Munich and Milan on the UEFA trail instead. Delia and I were gutted to miss out on the Olympic Stadium, but our magazine had been nominated for an award in London the same night. However we returned home at two in the morning well-fuelled by champagne (we won the award) and sat down to watch our recording of the match armed, if necessary, with more champagne. By the time dawn broke we were well over the moon and well over the limit. We also had the added pleasure of re-winding Jerry Goss's sledgehammer volley over and over.

Curiously the San Siro was a bit of an anti-climax. In a half-empty stadium the Yellow Army did its best to raise the temperature and spur the team to overcoming the 1-0 deficit.

God knows they tried, but the moment Dennis Bergkamp embarked on that breakaway down the left in the dying embers you knew it was over. Well, not quite. Our abiding memory is of waking up at three in the morning in our hotel near the station and hearing repeated choruses of On The Ball City ringing out over the city. It almost made the journey worthwhile.

The sorry unfolding of events in 1996 is part of Canary folklore. The year began with a state of outright hostility between fans and chairman Robert Chase: he pointing out that under his aegis the club had enjoyed its greatest sustained success, they disillusioned with the subsequent exodus of treasured players and managers, and the mounting debts brought on by what seemed unnecessary expenditure (did we really need monogrammed carpets in the City stand, or our own radio station on match days?). In spite of that we still stood a comfortable seventh in the Premier at the turn of the year.

A few weeks later Delia and I happened to bump into Chase on the train to London just after we had just dumped Coventry out of the cup. In spite of an already ominous slide down the table he was in bullish mood. Only two more wins were needed for safety, he explained, and then went on, without a hint of irony, to outline his hopes for floating the club on the stock market. The truth is that, apart from beating a virtually relegated, ten-man Ipswich side, we failed to win any of our last 19 games. Add to that the fact that this was the season that four clubs, not three, were relegated (to bring the Premier down to 20) and the impossible became the inevitable.

SECOND HALF

So in one of those twists of footballing fate my first 40 years began and ended under the same dark clouds, with City struggling on the pitch and close to extinction off it. Back in

1956 the crisis was averted by a new board under Geoffrey Watling and a public fund orchestrated by Arthur South. In 1996 the issues were more complicated. The debts this time were in a different league, the club was in a state of civil war, and the bank would offer no leeway while the old regime was in place. Chase agreed to sell his shares but could come to no arrangement with the one or two consortia that had been hastily assembled. Finally the president, Geoffrey Watling, stepped in – yet again – and salvaged the wreckage with an undisclosed offer, which Chase accepted.

While this opened the door to a settlement, the crippling debt remained, of course. Martin Armstrong, chief executive of the Norwich and Peterborough Building Society, had joined the emergency board and was tirelessly scouring the City for any kind of help, but football clubs were definitely not flavour of the month with financial institutions just then; as they surveyed the wave of administrations lapping over the league (Hartlepool, Exeter, Gillingham, with Millwall and Bournemouth teetering on the brink). With a matter of days to spare Martin invited Delia and myself out to dinner (Thai, if you want to know) to ask if we could help. If we could make the required loan we would get two seats on the board. We'd think about it, we said.

So we did for a few minutes. We thought of all the things we would prefer to do with the money than help to safeguard Norwich City's future and, do you know, we couldn't come up with a single one, even though we honestly never expected to see the cash again. That was a conclusion reinforced by our very first board meeting: the scale of the economies was draconian – redundancies and job-sharing throughout the club, all meals for the squad at Colney cancelled, no expenditure over £5 permitted unless signed off by the new chief executive, Gordon Bennett... and so it went on.

A year later, with Geoffrey Watling well into his eighties and in indifferent health, we were urged by Martin Armstrong to try to buy his shareholding, which proved easier said than done. Courteous as ever, Geoffrey invited Delia and myself to dinner, served us with sherry and escorted us into his study. Facing him across an enormous desk, containing a solitary notepad, it felt for all the world like an interview with the headmaster (which I suppose it was in a way). We mentioned a figure, he scribbled a note, then stood up impassively and said 'let us dine'. Was that all then? As it happened, yes it was, apart from a tour of his Norwich City museum at the top of the house, which contained among many other things ancient and forgotten trophies, a gilded music-box with a revolving canary on top and – most perplexing of all – silver replicas of Duncan Forbes' football boots.

Then he went off on a cruise, but not before writing to inform us he was not selling his shares at this time. So we were staggered to receive another letter a week or two later saying he would sell the shares to us after all. The reasons for this change of heart he took to his grave, but we remained on excellent terms with him for the rest of his life.

On the field Norwich were still struggling to play their way out of the bottom half of the division; off the field the finances were, if anything, even more precarious. The board's response was to sanction the issue of a shedful of more shares and to embark on a one-for-one share subscription. For legal reasons (Norwich City at that time being a private company) this was restricted to existing shareholders who, in effect, would have to buy their shares all over again to maintain their percentage shareholding – which included ourselves as newly-fledged 30 per cent shareholders!

In what feels in retrospect like a somewhat cavalier moment Delia and I also agreed to underwrite the share issue, and hope that enough of the other shareholders would take the altruistic view and pay up.

In the event many did, but quite a few, including some with significant shareholdings, did not and the unforeseen outcome was that by the end of 1998 our own percentage had increased to 63 per cent! It has always been an article of faith with us that a football club, any football club, belongs to the fans and that owners and directors are at best only trustees and caretakers for a finite period – though I appreciate this may not be the universal view among Russian oligarchs, American entrepreneurs or Middle Eastern sheikhs. Nonetheless it is a sobering thought that a lifetime on the terraces does not automatically qualify you to run a football club or to be immune from mistakes, and there were a few of them!

When Mike Walker left after two seasons that never threatened to match his first tenure, the board decided to interview and do due-diligence on at least 14 candidates (there may have been more but we lost count). There were plenty of familiar faces among them and, as you might expect, each one of them had something of his own to contribute – apart from one who turned up along with his agent as if negotiations could start on the spot. It was a protracted and unenlightening process, tantalisingly nurturing the hope that next time Supermanager would come crashing though the door. He didn't of course, and we swore never to repeat the process. In the end the board were obliged to hold a formal ballot of the directors – the only time I can recall that happening in 20 years – and Bruce Rioch duly arrived in his custom-registered car R1 OCH.

Running a football club, we very soon discovered, is like running no other business in the world: conventional models go out of the window. Market forces may still apply but nowhere else are they subject to such unpredictables as injuries and refereeing decisions, or such intangibles as 'losing the dressing-room'. We were very fortunate to be able to spend time learning from the likes of Roy Hodgson and Bobby Robson (then with Barcelona) and even Guy Roux, the legendary coach at Auxerre whose edicts included the rule that his players should only ever drink water – and that in spite of Auxerre's principal sponsor being the leading Chablis producer in the region!

It was patently obvious that the club needed to revisit some basic principles, one of which was that the principal purpose of the club was football, not business. But without a healthy commercial base there would be no football, and so countless hours were spent debating the merits of a club shop in Castle Mall, in identifying new sponsors, and in restructuring the kitchens and creating new restaurants, which gave rise to dark mutterings among fans and journalists that we were more interested in hot-plates than points. But the fact of the matter was that before long the catering operation was contributing the best part of £1million to the squad, and now rather more.

Meanwhile the flirtation with relegation continued. When Bryan Hamilton, who had briefly succeeded Rioch, fell on his sword at the beginning of December 2000 City were 20th in the table. His natural successor was Nigel Worthington, his assistant manager, but somewhat cautiously the board gave him just six matches over the Christmas period to make an impact. Armed with two wins and three draws in the New Year though, he presented a persuasive case for leading City to safety, as indeed he did. His first full season, however, began with a 4-0 mullering away at Millwall and the expectations raised by an unusually good pre-season melted away. But this was Norwich, don't forget, and as I recall we won the next four games without conceding a goal, which sent the stattos diving for their record books.

They would have been at it again for the final match of

the season, with the Canaries in seventh place but on the same points as Burnley in sixth and just one goal behind on goal difference. You could touch the tension in the ground as we kicked off for our game with Stockport, only slightly eased when their goalie was sent off in the second minute. Then word came through that Burnley had scored – hell and damnation! But then Phil Mulryne puts us ahead in the second half – blessed relief! Finally Malky cracks one past the deputy goalkeeper – bliss beyond compare – and the whistle goes with City in the play-offs.

But hang on. They are still playing at Turf Moor and Paul Gascoigne, no less, is about to take a free kick on the edge of the area, deep into injury time. The silence around Carrow Road is stifling, a frozen tableau of faces, with trannies sealed to ears. Suddenly, bedlam. Gazza's low free kick has been tipped round the post!

The subsequent passage to the Millennium Stadium was no less fraught, in particular the final buttock-clenching 15 minutes at Molineux as City desperately defended their one-goal lead against Wolves, but we survived.

On May 12th, then, convoy after convoy of balloon-festooned cars crossed the Severn Bridge and converged on Cardiff. Three hours before kick-off every street leading to the Norwich end of the stadium was a raucous sea of green and yellow as far as the eye could see, one of the most emotional sights – Delia and I agreed – we had ever witnessed.

In those days the play-off final was not yet billed as the Richest Match In The World (though it probably was), because the truly eye-watering rewards were still over the horizon, but it did strike us as something of an anomaly that the winner should qualify for their share of the takings on top of the millions they would earn from the Premier League. In the minutes leading up to the kick-off our chief executive, Neil

Doncaster, circumvented the Football League and reached an arrangement with the Gold brothers at Birmingham that the winning side would cede its share to the losers. It is a precedent followed ever since.

In the event that did nothing to assuage the desolation of losing the penalty shoot-out, nor dampen the fire-fighting that was now a constant feature of board meetings. The sale of some land for development and a moderately successful public share issue helped to stabilise the squad for the time being, but a report at the beginning of 2003 that the South Stand – the only original structure left – was to all intents and purposes condemned and would cost a fortune simply to get a safety certificate came as a body-blow.

To pay for a new stand the board voted to seek a 'secu-ratisation' from Axa. In other words, a mortgage secured on future season-ticket sales – a form of loan that had previously only been offered to Premier League clubs. It was a calculated risk but one that appeared to be paying off when, even as the spanking new Jarrold Stand opened its doors for business in February 2004, the team were cementing a five-point lead at the top of Division One (as what is now the Championship was then called). When we clinched the title away at Sunderland – even though we lost – the friendship forged between the clubs in 1985 at Wembley was reaffirmed when they broke open the champagne.

There was more champagne to follow in July when, courtesy of our sponsors Proton, the team landed in Kuala Lumpur for a pre-season tour in Malaysia, (a far cry from playing friendlies on rugby pitches in Ireland, which is what had occurred soon after Delia and I joined the board). It was so hot that the players were told to immerse themselves in barrels of ice after training, apart from one (nameless) who refused to take that option under any circumstances. Hundreds of Canary fans painted the city centre green and yellow, along with hundreds more locals whom they had recruited into a newly-formed Malaysian supporters club. For the board rather more diplomacy was required. At a regal banquet hosted by the Crown Prince we noticed that the only settings without wine glasses were ours and his. We did not summon the wine-waiter to complain!

However, beware the beautiful game. Norwich were warmly welcomed back into the Premier, because we were a team who 'liked to play football', or was it because we might be easy pickings?, you just couldn't tell. For most of the season we were both, until a wonderful rally at the end left us only needing to win our final game to stay in the Premier. I can hardly bear to dwell on that 6-0 capitulation at Craven Cottage but for the fact that it had such far-reaching consequences. It was as if a set of dominoes was collapsing: relegation fomenting a hangover that spread from the pitch to the terraces, leading to protest marches and vitriol on the message-boards – PS, no, we didn't filch the money.

What money anyway? Now the loan repayments were weighing down on the club like a millstone, and with no prospect whatsoever of any further corporate backing there only remained the directors to throw a lifeline. Mike Foulger (who has invariably stepped up to the plate in times of crisis over the past 20 years), Andrew and Sharon Turner and we ourselves provided the funds to keep the club's head above water.

Not surprisingly the vultures were now circling. There was no shortage of opportunists offering 'to take the debt off our hands' armed with the romantic notion that they could negotiate it down with Axa. Delia and I issued a statement – somewhat against our better judgment – that we wouldn't rule out foreign investment if it were in the club's best interests, but there was a deafening silence from Dubai and Wall Street.

One credible suitor, however, appeared with the zealous backing of a local paper. Peter Cullum had made a huge reputation in the City by bucking the financial trends and hoovering up scores of small companies into his megalithic Towergate Partnership. Via the press he offered 'to put £20million into the squad' in return for ownership, though this does not entirely accord with our recollection of discussions with him. It proved irrelevant anyway, because at our last meeting the bid was withdrawn, which may or may not have had anything to do with the fact that by then he was reported to have other financial issues on his mind.

Three managerial departures, Nigel Worthington, Peter Grant and Glenn Roeder, over the next two-and-a-half years underlined the increasingly tenuous grip City had on the Championship (as it had become). The *coup de grace* came on May 3rd 2009 at Charlton, who had themselves already been relegated, and we found ourselves back in the third tier of English football for the first time in 50 years and facing the imminent arrival of the administrators.

If Delia and I, and every other fan, thought this was the worst day of our lives, there was worse to follow. But in the meantime two straws appeared within our grasp. First, our amazing supporters rallied to the cause by purchasing more season tickets than ever before, and secondly in the inevitable restructuring that had to follow relegation, we were able to appoint – persuade might be more appropriate – Alan Bowkett as chairman and David McNally as chief executive.

If they had misgivings about the task ahead these could only have deepened on the opening day of the new season when 4-0 down to Colchester after 20 minutes saw supporters tearing up their season-tickets in front of poor Bryan Gunn.

The final 7-1 scoreline was undoubtedly the nadir, the least wanted record of all time... but also it turned out to be the ashes from which a phoenix might yet rise.

Alan, whose reputation in the City went before him, some-how convinced our creditors of the benefits of a moratorium on interest and a restructuring of capital repayments that would give the club breathing space. David, tapping into a profound knowledge of the game honed at Celtic and Fulham, found and installed Paul Lambert as manager, the very man who had inflicted the 7-1 defeat on us! How inspired this appointment was rapidly dawned on us as the Canaries flew from rock bottom of the league to displacing a rampant Leeds at the top by mid-January, and never looked back.

As it happens Delia and I found our acquaintance with the third tier of the game very refreshing. We were a million miles from the plush boardrooms of the Premier, with their waiters in white gloves and food supposedly finer than the proverbial prawn sandwiches. Apart from the opportunity to visit grounds we had never set foot in (and even coming away with points), we were lucky to get to know so many directors who are the backbone of league football in this country – the very antithesis of Simon Jordan's description of some boardroom incumbents as 'tossers drinking Chardonnay'. Here were life-long fans of their club, rooted in the community, struggling from game to game with the financial inequalities of lower-league football. It certainly helped to put our own issues into a wider context.

Back in the Championship the phoenix completed its ascent at Portsmouth on the evening of May 2nd 2011, when the news greeted us at Fratton Park that our nearest rivals Cardiff had imploded in their early game and a win would seal promotion. It seemed an eternity before Simeon Jackson headed his ninth goal in seven games. It was ten years since any team had achieved back-to-back promotions to the Premier-ship. The roars rang around Norfolk and probably around a few accountants' offices as well.

By now the external debt, with accrued interest, topped £25million, but two relatively settled years in the Premier and prudent housekeeping saw it paid off in full, every penny of it. But equally important for us has been to keep enshrined the principles of 'football and community first'. One immediate target was to achieve Category One status for the Academy under the new regulations, which clearly paid off when, much to Chelsea's irritation, the under-18s won the FA Youth Cup. Recruitment, sports science, analysis, nutrition, all of which had once seemed something of a luxury, are now top of the agenda. The club's Community Sports Foundation – which has worked unsung wonders in schools, with the homeless, the old, the very young and those with disabilities – gains momentum each year.

EXTRA TIME

When I started writing these random recollections I wondered how they would end up. Delia and I scarcely dared to believe I would be able to conclude with what I have no doubt is the greatest day in the club's history.

Some may say we are simply basking in the euphoria of having won a play-off final, others may argue the case for earlier triumphs recounted here – 'The 1959 Cup Run', the Milk Cup, Bayern Munich.

But consider the context of the 2015 Wembley victory: the inspirational surge up the table under Alex Neil (unbeaten away in 12 consecutive matches), the small matter of defeating Ipswich in the semi-finals, the global audience of hundreds of millions, the awesome rewards at stake and, above all, the manner of the victory. Even to our untutored eyes the tactics and quality of the football were immaculate. Even the Boro fans, so gracious in defeat, made the day unforgettable.

Anyone who has shared a glass of wine with Delia and myself from time to time will know – even to the point of boredom – we have one recurring toast. It is not to the richest, most galactic, most trophy-laden club in the world; it is to, in all the things that give football its heart, 'the best football club in the world'.

Michael Wynn Jones has been a writer, editor and publisher. His 40 years as an 'ordinary' Norwich supporter have been followed by two decades (so far) in the boardroom, alongside his wife, Delia Smith.

3

Iwan Roberts tells us about the men who played alongside him during seven memorable years at the City.

We learn about Craig Bellamy's boasts, Craig Fleming's snoring and Darren Huckerby's training.

And along the way he reveals a lot about himself – how he feels he let down Mike Walker and just how hard he had to work to shape-up before establishing himself as a goalscorer supreme and one of the club's all-time greats.

NOT THE WORST, AFTER ALL

BY IWAN ROBERTS

My last game at Carrow Road ended with me fighting back the tears as the crowd chanted, 'Iwan! Iwan! Iwan!'. But my Norwich career didn't start like that. At the very beginning, the chant was, 'What a waste of money'. And in the letters page of the *Eastern Daily Press*, one person said I was the worst player the club had ever signed. Another went further, saying I was the worst ever to wear a Norwich shirt. It was the bleakest period of all my years as a pro.

I hadn't even wanted to join Norwich – or rather, I hadn't wanted to leave Wolves. I'd only been there for a season and I had another two years left on my contract. It was late June 1997. Mark McGhee, the Wolves manager, called me into his office on the first day of pre-season. I had arrived back from Australia the day before, having spent the whole of my time off over the summer there. Mark didn't mess about in telling me that he had accepted an offer from another club for my services. I told him I didn't really want to leave, but he'd been told that before he could bring in any new faces he had to sell players first – and I was the only player that an offer had been made for!

He told me to go and talk to Mike Walker, the Norwich boss, and look around at Carrow Road and the training ground at Colney, and if I then didn't fancy the move to come back and fight for my place. But I was not stupid. I had been in the game long enough to realise that if the club had accepted an offer for me, and the manager was okay about that, then he was basically telling me I wasn't in his plans. I had no future at Wolves.

So the very next morning I set off to Norwich with my then agent David Speedie (who I'd played alongside at Leicester) to have a look around the place and discuss terms. The first thing that hits you when travelling to Norwich is how far from everywhere the place is. After you've lived in Norfolk for a while you realise that's a positive and not a negative. But that journey, with so much going through my mind, seemed to last for ever. The negotiations didn't take long, however. Mike showed us around, and David did the deal about personal terms while I was having my medical with Tim Sheppard.

Everything was agreed and obviously I was impressed with the facilities at both the ground and the training ground, which was nearly brand new, but I still wanted to think things over. I had to be 100 per cent sure about the move. However, after a weekend of thinking about things long and hard I decided that my future lay in Norfolk. Mind you, I still pulled into a lay-by near Snetterton to ask myself if I was doing the right thing. Yet once the season kicked off, just about everyone else had doubts about whether signing me was right. Mike had described me as 'the final piece of the jigsaw' – but I fell apart in the box. Boom, tish!

Off the pitch, I just couldn't settle. I honestly don't know why but I found it so hard. I had to stay at the Holiday Inn on the Ipswich Road. I wanted my son Ben to start school in the area in September and so he stayed with me while his mum and his twin sister stayed in Shropshire. That wasn't ideal. Don't get me wrong: staying in a nice hotel for a couple of weeks is lovely, but when you are there for nearly five months you hanker for a home. There was a nice lad who used to serve me breakfast, though – the one and only Jake Humphrey, a Norwich fan and now a television presenter – who had a part-time job there.

On the pitch, I couldn't get going. Breakfasts might have been part of my problem. I was slightly heavier than I should have been, because I had not done much training while away in Australia. The club had forked out a hefty £850,000 for me, so supporters were expecting big things, but perhaps not quite that big. It was a tough time for me and I took some stick, which is never nice, but I could totally understand the fans' frustrations with my lack of good performances and even more importantly lack of goals. I scored home and away in the two-legged League Cup tie against Barnet in August and I remember my first league goal against Middlesbrough – a header from a peach of a cross from Danny Mills – but that wasn't until November, and we lost that Middlesbrough game, at home.

Goals that season were few and far between. I heard the shouts. They were things like, 'Why don't you go back to Wolves, Roberts you donkey?' There were plenty more, but you have to keep your head down, work hard, not let the doubters win and try and prove people wrong. I don't know why, but I read the letters pages in the *Eastern Daily Press* and the *Evening News* to see what people were writing about me, and believe you me, none of it was good.

The incident that really hurt me though came when I walked out of the players' entrance with my son Ben after we had lost another home game. I had performed shockingly. The players' entrance was at the Barclay End. As we turned to walk down Carrow Road we were met by around 50 fans who had been protesting at the main entrance of the City Stand. As soon as they saw me they vented their anger. They swore, they booed, they called me all sorts of things, but instead of turning round and heading straight back into the safety of the players' bar I headed straight for them. It wasn't pleasant and boy was I relieved to reach my car. As soon as we got into the car Ben turned to me and asked, 'Dad why don't those men like you?'

For him to have to go through that at four years of age was wrong, but it made me so determined from that moment on to show everyone that I was not a waste of money or the worst signing the club had ever made.

That season finished better for me with three goals in the final two home games. That won some fans over but I knew that I would have to come back fitter, leaner and hungrier the following season if I was to convince the majority of supporters. Those goals were not enough to save my good friend Mike Walker from being sacked, and to this day I still hold myself massively responsible for his departure. He had put so much faith in signing me and I let him down badly.

My second season at Norwich was by far my best for the club and I have Bruce Rioch to thank for that. Oh and a certain Welshman. Well he was more of a boy at the time: Craig Bellamy.

As a player, when a new man takes charge you're always a bit in limbo. You don't know whether you're going to be his type of player or not. You don't know if you still have a future at the club or if you will be moved. But Bruce had tried to sign me a couple of times when he had been in charge at Bolton, so when he got the Norwich job that summer, I was quietly confident and looking forward to working with him. It didn't take too long before the doubts started to creep in, though.

In fact, a simple sentence from Bruce was all it took for me to realise that I had to sort myself out or I would be on the footballing scrapheap at the grand old age of 30. It was in Bruce's first meeting with everyone up in the dining room at Colney, when he was being introduced to us all, that the bombshell was dropped. All the players had been in early for all their fitness tests and to be weighed. We had been off for over two months. But, unlike the summer before, I had worked reasonably hard through the break. Yet I still found myself a bit over weight. Well, nearly a stone over to be exact. Bruce was a no-nonsense, old-school type of a manager and I liked that, but he was far from impressed with my results, especially how heavy I'd come back.

In front of everyone, he pulled his glasses down to the tip of his nose, looked at the piece of paper in his hand with my results on it, then looked up at me and, in a quiet voice, said, 'Iwan, Tom Walley would be very proud of you!'

Those simple words gave me the biggest kick up the back-side ever and I instantly realised that I was drinking in the last chance saloon. Why was I so shocked at what Bruce had said? It's not as if he'd ranted and raved at me. To be fair, I wish he had. It would have been easier to take.

Bruce was being sarcastic with his comment about Tom Walley, who was my youth team coach at Watford and probably the biggest influence in my career. He'd worked with Bruce at both Millwall and Arsenal, so they knew each other very well. Tom was a fitness fanatic and wanted his players to be the same. He hated any player who was overweight and not looking after himself properly. Bruce knew that Tom would have been appalled by my condition. I knew it too.

There and then I knew I had to get to grips with myself, lose the excess weight I was carrying and get myself into the best shape of my life. Fortunately, the right manager was in place for that. Bruce's pre-seasons were well known in the game for being absolute killers. So the Norwich players were expecting a tough time and their expectations were fulfilled. I've completed 21 pre-seasons and that one was by far the toughest I've ever encountered. It was exactly what I needed, because it did the trick. Three sessions a day and the weight dropped off. I lost a stone and a half and was the fittest I'd ever been.

I was on the bench when the season started, though. The manager opted for the youth of Bellamy and Keith O'Neil up front for the opening fixture, a League Cup match at Swansea, and they played very well, causing the defence problems with their pace and movement. I just had to be patient.

In the first league game, away to Stockport, Keith picked up an injury and I replaced him with six minutes left. Keith was back in the team for the next match: the second leg against Swansea in the League Cup. He came off at the stroke of 90 minutes. I went on – and scored after 91! But there still wasn't a sniff of a place in the starting line-up for me.

Then, in the sixth game of the season, we lost 2-0 at West Brom. This time it was Darren Eadie I replaced as sub 18 minutes from time, and I think it was the fact that I was so determined and focused every time I got off the bench, that persuaded Bruce to give me a proper go. Or, more accurately, it was the fact that Keith was having real injury problems that meant I was in the starting line-up for the game at Barnsley on a Tuesday night in early September. It's not the ideal way to get into the team when a team-mate gets injured, but it's part of the game. I felt bad for Keith, as he was a great lad who I'd got on with from day one.

But that Tuesday night at Barnsley we won. I scored and so did Bellars. A partnership had begun. We hit it off on the pitch straight away and I can't really explain to you why. Yes, we are both passionate Welshmen but that's all we really had in common, because he was closer to my son's age than to mine. So when I invited him round to the house for tea he'd spend more time on the PlayStation with Ben than he would talking to me.

On the pitch, though, it was as if the understanding between us was telepathic. I knew exactly what he was going to do and where he wanted the ball and vice-versa. I loved playing up front with him, even if he could be a mouthy git at times! He was scary quick and was so confident for such a young lad. He knew he was going to reach the very top. Some people thought

Craig was arrogant and, well, he probably was, but it didn't really bother me because he could back it up with his performances and I've always thought that all the top players have that little bit of arrogance about them. That's what makes them the players they are.

Now, don't get me wrong: I've fallen out with Bellars more than once. I remember on one night out in Ireland, where we were on pre-season tour, having a proper argument with him. I'd overheard him saying something about me to one of the other players. I responded with, 'Shut up, you one season wonder'. Boy, did those words come back to haunt me! But to this day we laugh about it and if we had our fallings out, it never affected how we were with each other on the field. That's how it should be.

It wasn't all rows though. I was quite protective of Craig, as he mentions in his autobiography. He was a fantastic player too and I firmly believe that if he not received an horrendous injury at the hands – or rather the feet – of a certain Kevin Muscat at Wolves, we wouldn't have been far off winning promotion that season. I heard the crack of Craig's kneecap as Muscat clattered Craig and I knew that he would be out for a long period. Bruce came storming onto the pitch in a fury about the challenge. Norwich fans never forgave Muscat or his club, Wolves. And the injury caused Craig problems for the rest of his career.

The injury happened in early December. Craig and I had scored more goals than any other strike partnership at the club, and without the injury I think we could have scored enough goals to fire us towards the top of the division. But Craig didn't play again until the end of January – after very nearly two months. It was a long, disruptive absence. I ended up that season with 23 goals, 19 of which came in the league. I was gutted that I didn't reach the magical 20 league goals mark which all forwards set themselves at the start of the season, but I won the Barry Butler Player Of The Season trophy. And fans had started chanting my name, instead of, 'What a waste of money!'

Bellars was one of the two best trainers at the club in my seven years there. The other was another extremely talented player: Darren Huckerby. Bellars and Hucks would both go out every morning and train as if it were their last ever session. They both prepared meticulously before training, to make sure they were warmed up properly and ensure they could commit to whatever session that was planned for us.

They had other similarities too. They were both were electrifyingly quick and ultra competitive. Hucks still is, now we're both over 35 and play vets football. When Hucks and I played in the first Jamie's Game, for the Norwich City Community Sports Foundation, at Carrow Road, I played at centre-back and had a bit of fun, as befitted the occasion. Hucks wanted to win, believe me. He was very upset about being asked to swap sides because he had scored so many for the first side they'd stuck him in! I haven't played with Craig for years, but I can't imagine that Craig has lost any of his competitive edge either, because he had so much of it.

I would have loved to have played more games with Darren because I know he would have made sure he created enough chances for me to score over 100 goals for the club (instead of the 96 I finished on). Hucks was such an unselfish player and that's the only difference between him and Bellars. Hucks would get as much pleasure in creating a goal as he would in scoring a goal whereas Craig wouldn't. Craig was more selfish. He would rather try and score himself than pass to a team-mate who was in a better position to score ... but I've done that myself on a few occasions.

Hucks and I have stayed good friends over the years and I've a massive amount of respect for him as a person and for what he did for Norwich City. If it wasn't for him joining us on loan and then signing for us at Christmas 2003, we would never have won the Football League. It's as simple as that. We had a decent side that might have made the play-offs, but Darren gave us that something different, that X-factor that any side needs if they have ambitions of winning titles. I didn't collect too many medals in my career. I got a couple of play-off winners' medals with Leicester, but the one that takes pride of place in my son's bedroom is my Championship winners medal from the 2003-04 season. And I've Hucks to thank for that.

Perhaps my lucky pants played a part too. I'm quite a superstitious person and had so many things that I had to go through before a game on a Saturday, especially if I'd scored the week before. I had a routine at home and it rarely changed. In the morning, I'd take the dog for a walk at nine, sit down relax and watch a bit of TV before having my pre-match meal at about eleven. I'd get changed into my club suit at noon and put on the same pants as the week before if I'd scored. That's how superstitious I was.

I always liked to get to Carrow Road at about one o'clock to make sure I was in before the 1.30pm deadline so I wouldn't get fined. No seriously, I was always early because I don't like rushing around and leaving things until the last minute. Obviously the routine was different for away games when we were staying in hotels, but the one thing that would never change, home or away, was the fact that I had to be third or fourth out of the changing room, and I always put my left boot on last. Don't ask me why, as I've no idea!

I wasn't keen on away games because of all the travelling, lots of time to kill, sleeping in a bed that's alien to you and, worst of all, having to share a hotel room with a team-mate! To be fair, the lads who had the pleasure of my company in hotels during my time at Norwich were all very good to share with –

apart from one. Craig Fleming was a shocking room partner. Flem and I signed in the same week back in 1997 and we've remained good friends ever since but, dear me, sharing a hotel room with him tested that friendship.

With Flem it was lights out at no later than nine at night. I kid you not! If I wanted the telly on after lights out, it couldn't be louder than number two on the volume control, which Flem would set with the remote control before he went to sleep. Believe you me, he would wake up straight away if I dared turn the volume up to level three. And while I was being careful with the noise, Flem was snoring louder than any human I have ever encountered. That was the fault of all the elbows he'd taken to the face in all his years of playing. His nose had taken such a battering that he couldn't breathe through it properly. So he snored. And snored. Loudly.

My award for the best room-mate has to go to Darryl Sutch. He was a great lad and not only a very good room-mate but a fantastic Hearts partner. Hearts is the card game we spent hours playing at the back of the coach while on long away journeys. Yes Sutchy and I lost a few but we won far more than we lost. It was a great way of passing the time on long coach trips on a Friday afternoon. And, as fans who go to away games know, the journeys can be really, really long.

I made more than 150 of those trips as a Norwich player – and this was long before the Elveden by-pass, don't forget. Trips back were a lot more bearable if we'd won, and even more so if I had scored. City fans often ask me which was the best or favourite goal I scored for the club. They are often surprised I don't pick the one against Birmingham in the play-off final at Cardiff in 2002, although I suppose that wasn't a bad one!

'Small' McVeigh swept a really good, cross-field ball to Alex Notman, who cut in from the right and sent over a fabulous ball to beyond the far post, where I was ready for it. Big Ron

Atkinson was co-commentating on the game on TV and he described my contact as a textbook header. I'll settle for that.

For a split second it was the most important goal I'd ever scored, as I thought it had won us the game. It was in extra-time, and I thought we were playing to the 'golden goal' system, which meant the first goal in extra-time wins the game. But after getting off the floor after celebrating with the lads I turned around and realised Stern John and Geoff Horsfield were ready to restart the game. We obviously weren't using the golden goal!

I was gutted. And, as we all know they equalised and then we lost on penalties. I scored my pen, though and it was just a shame I couldn't take all five! No, I used to hate taking penalties, and I hated how that game in Cardiff was decided. I'd never cried on a football pitch, but I did that day. I was sat on the pitch, head between my knees, having to stay out there and watch Birmingham celebrate their victory. It is still the biggest disappointment in my career. I thought at the time that there was no chance at my age that I would get another crack at the Premier League, and how right I was.

So what was my best goal for the club? I remember a sweet strike at Oakwell when we wore that 'lovely' dark blue kit with fluorescent yellow patches on it. And, of course, there was that left-footed strike against Crewe in my final game for the club. That was a special one, but not my best.

My best goal for City came on March 19th, 2000, against Ipswich Town at Portman Road. I never lost an East Anglian derby in my time at the club but this game against the Old Enemy was by far my most enjoyable. We won 2-0 in Bryan Hamilton's first game in charge as manager with what was probably our best performance of that season. To make things even better, I scored both goals. My first took a slight deflection but there was nothing lucky about the second.

It came from their corner kick. Andy Marshall (still playing for us then) caught the ball and threw it out to the right to Paul Dalglish – who hadn't inherited his old man's skills but boy was he quick. He must have got his pace from his mum! Anyway, Paul tore down that right-hand side and crossed an inch-perfect cross to the far post. I took three touches. With the first I controlled the ball on my thigh and Fabian Wilnis so misread what was happening that he kept going so far past me that I thought he'd gone for a pie. My second touch stopped the ball dead so I could steady myself, and my killer third touch planted the ball firmly to the left of Richard Wright. Even if I say so myself, it was a quality goal. It has been likened to one Dennis Bergkamp scored against Leicester for Arsenal, which is high praise indeed. Personally, I think mine was better.

The only thing that spoilt that day was Bryan Hamilton in the dressing room afterwards telling us not to celebrate too loudly and to be gracious in victory. I've heard of being gracious in defeat but never in victory, especially against Ipswich Town. Bryan was a former favourite at Portman Road as a player and was still very popular down there, so I could understand him telling us what he did. But we ignored the instruction. Believe you me we made plenty of noise in the away dressing room. Folk who didn't get to that game probably heard us all the way up the A140 in Norwich.

Even though I scored two goals that day I wasn't man of the match, and rightly so. Our best player that day was the one and only Mike Milligan. He had by far his best game for the club. Mind you, that's not setting the bar very high! No, seriously, Milly was immense that day, as he reminds me every time we see each other. I didn't really get on with Milly when I first signed because I didn't know how to take him. He was the biggest mickey-taker in the dressing room and how I didn't punch him during those first couple of years God only knows.

He would slaughter you for anything and he wouldn't let you get a word in edgeways. He'd just talk over you.

It took a while for me to realise that it was all meant in fun, but eventually we became very close friends. Mike will do anything for you and that hasn't changed since we both stopped playing football.

Another Irishman I got on well with was Paul McVeigh. In this book I gather he says he was bought to play alongside me, but didn't know who I was when he joined. But I didn't know anything about him either, because I hadn't played much reserve team football! He signed on a free transfer from Spurs. I'd never heard of a free transfer before, so he had to explain to me what one was! You could tell, when you saw him with the ball at his feet, that he'd had his footballing education at Tottenham and these days I understand he turns out for the Tottenham Legends team. He must have made some impact then in his one appearance for Spurs in the third round of the League Cup in 1998! Sorry, Macca. The truth is I loved playing alongside you, because you were very good.

There were lots of good players during my Norwich years, and lots of very good times. But my time at the club ended, of course, and not as I had hoped.

I remember the day when I was told that my City career was over as if it was yesterday. It was April 29th, 2004. I received a phone call from Val Lemmon, Nigel Worthington's secretary, early on that Thursday morning, asking if I could come to the training ground at 8.30 as Nigel and Dougie Livermore wanted a meeting with me. Val didn't say what it was about, but she didn't have to. I knew there was only one thing that they wanted to talk to me about.

My contract finished on June 30th and I always hoped that I would be given another year but there had been no discussions. So now it was time to see what the future had in store for me.

If I'm honest, as I drove to Colney that morning, deep down I knew what Nigel was going to say. If he and the club wanted me to stay for another year it would have been sorted out before now. I walked into Nigel's office and both he and Dougie had very serious looks on their faces. That was another sign that there was going to be no eighth year at Norwich for me.

I sat down. Dougie cracked a joke to ease the tension, which was something he was good at. Then, all of a sudden, Nigel just came out with it. 'Robbo we've thought long and hard about this and it's the hardest decision I've ever had to make but the club won't be offering you another contract. So you will be given a free transfer at the end of June.'

I was 36 but I was a very fit 36 – ask Dave Carolan, our sports scientist and fitness coach at the time. I'd only started 13 games that season and I'd scored eight goals. I'd been involved in 41 of our 46 games, so I thought I'd earned another season and a crack at the Premier League. I certainly didn't want to be given a new contract for sentimental reasons. And I'm not stupid, I knew I wasn't going to start every game, but I think I could have been a good option to come off the bench if we were chasing a game with say 20-25 minutes to go.

So I was gutted by the club's decision, but I respected it, and at the end of the day that's football. Nigel gave his reasons. To this day I don't agree with any of them! But, just for the record, I don't hold any grudges against him at all. He had a job to do and decisions to make and he made them for the good of Norwich City. I really enjoyed working and playing under him and would class him still as a very good friend.

I managed to say all the right things at the time. I didn't want to spoil what was going to be a great last two weeks of the season for the club. But deep down I was hurting, of course.

My final game at Carrow Road came two days later, against Preston, and what an emotional day it was; one I'll never forget.

The news had broken that I was leaving after seven years and that this was going to be my farewell performance at Carrow Road. The reception I had when I came on that day was unbelievable. I'd never heard my name shouted so loudly. I was desperate to score and Hucks was as desperate to create me one and he came within inches of doing just that but I just couldn't quite reach his cross-come-shot before it crossed the line.

After the game we went into the dressing room but knew we would be going back out to do our traditional lap of honour and thank our fans for the fantastic support they'd given us all season. I was told to stay in the dressing room as all the rest of the lads and staff went out, and was left wondering what on earth was going on. But then I was told to head out. As I left the dressing room, there waiting for me were my three children Ben, Eva and Chase. I could tell by their eyes that they had been crying which really upset me. As we walked down the tunnel I could see the lads had formed a guard of honour for me and I thought that was a great touch from a fantastic bunch of lads who were like brothers to me.

I had to fight back the tears as we made our way towards the River End but managed to contain myself as 'Iwan! Iwan!' was chanted from all four corners of Carrow Road. I'd bought my shirt that I'd worn that day out with me, and there was only one place it was going: straight into the middle of the Barclay End. The players walked slowly around the stadium and, when we reached the Barclay, I untied the shirt from around my waist and threw it as far as I could into the crowd, I couldn't think of a better place for my shirt to go in my final home appearance for the club.

I signed for Gillingham as player-coach but didn't really enjoy my time in Kent. I loved working with Andy Hessenthaler but my heart wasn't really in it anymore. My desire had deserted me after I'd left Norwich and so I retired the following season and began working for BBC Wales as a pundit and have been doing this for the last nine years. I love my media work but I have got to know the roads to Wales rather well because I still live in the Fine City of Norwich. Of course.

Iwan Roberts not only needs no introduction, he doesn't need his surname. Just saying 'Iwan' is enough for City fans to conjure memories of the gap-toothed smile this all-time great produced after each of his 96 goals for the club.

4

One of his readers accused him of being an Ipswich fan but the Suffolk club's chairman called him Canary Boy.

The truth, as **Charlie Wyett** explains, is that he is yellow and green through and through.

His double life as a supporter and one of the nation's top football reporters has given him a unique view of the club and some of its managers.

Here he shares that view with us, and talks too of the difficulty of remaining professional when he cares so much about City.

TRYING TO BE NEUTRAL, NOT NEUTERED

BY CHARLIE WYETT

For the last 25 years, part of my job has been to mark footballers' performances out of ten so I cannot complain if a supporter critiques my work. If a football fan contacts me to stress my match report was absolute garbage, then I have to accept the criticism. It is part of the job. A thick skin helps.

Contacting a journalist is straightforward these days. Emails and Twitter mean there is an instant route of communication between sports fan and hack. But it is not that long ago when to get in touch with a journalist, either a letter or a telephone call to the office was required – and the comments from readers were rarely positive.

There was one particular writer, from Sweden, who would send me his comments and mark the envelope 'Charlie Wyett a sort of journalist' at *The Sun*.

On one occasion, I received a call at what was known as 'Fortress Wapping' – Rupert Murdoch's London base before we all moved to London Bridge. *The Sun*'s sports desk secretary rang my extension number, saying, 'Hi there, there's a lady on the phone who wants to speak to 'that shit reporter called Charlie,' can I put her through?'

This is how I remember the conversation:

WOMAN: Is that Charlie? I'm a Norwich fan and your football reports are rubbish. Your paper should not be allowing biased, Ipswich supporters anywhere near our games.

ME: I completely respect the fact if you think I am a bit rubbish but I do try and be objective in all my match reports.

WOMAN: Well, you're not.

ME: And secondly, the bit about me supporting Ipswich. Well, I sort of don't.

WOMAN: You do.

ME: Well, I don't.

WOMAN: You do. Definitely, I read your Ipswich stuff. It is obvious.

ME: If you must know, I actually support Norwich.

The woman thought I was humouring her. I then explained that although I had been sent to a lot of Ipswich matches – this was a long time ago, when they were quite good – my team was Norwich. I was from near Hunstanton, my first game as a fan was Wolves at home in 1978-79. But, that as a sports journalist, I did everything in my power to be objective while giving a comment about matches and the situations at any of the clubs I covered.

The woman accepted my point and we had a good laugh. Yet her comments did make me think about the issue of objectivity, particularly when you are involved in covering the club you care about.

The truth is that I always enjoyed covering Ipswich, despite the rivalry. It was well known among those I dealt with at Portman Road that I supported Norwich. A few others in the national media knew too, but it was seldom a problem.

When Ipswich were in the UEFA Cup in 2001-02, the journalists all sat at the back of the team's plane from Stansted on trips to Moscow, Sweden and Milan. They were good trips, and my Norfolk roots and affiliation did not cause any issues to Ipswich or for me.

The following season, when Ipswich had been relegated, they qualified for Europe again, courtesy of the UEFA Fair Play League, and there was mixed seating on a flight to Prague

for a match against Czech side Slovan Liberec. I found myself
seated next to Matt Holland, their captain at the time. As he
sat down, he said, 'Chirp, chirp' – making the point that he
was aware of my allegiances. Again, though, those allegiances
did not cause any problems after that greeting and, to this day,
David Sheepshanks, the former Ipswich chairman, calls me
'Canary Boy'.

If anything, I was not critical enough of Ipswich during that
season. They were struggling in the Championship and they fell
to pieces after making a string of ludicrous signings the previous season. Sub-consciously, perhaps I gave them an easy ride.

Of course, however objective we try to be in national newspapers, supporters of all clubs generally think they are being
hard done-by. Yet, in many respects, local journalists have a
tougher job than those of us on the nationals when it comes
to being objective. At the local level, most clubs believe that
'their' local newspaper, radio or TV station should generally
be positive. But if the team is not doing well, then supporters
expect the local media to share their frustration and anger. Fans
often demand that their local media, particularly newspapers,
should be as critical as the people on the terraces. In those circumstances, the clubs expect support from the local press and
the fans demand criticism. Usually, both camps are unhappy.

My first experience covering teams as a local reporter was
at the *Cambs Times* and my teams were March Town United and
Chatteris Town. Both were playing in the Premier Division of
the Eastern Counties League.

The people in March felt I favoured Chatteris. Yet down
the road at Chatteris, they were convinced I favoured March.
The truth was, though, that my favourite non-League team was
King's Lynn. As far as the great March-Chatteris divide was
concerned, I was completely neutral.

But one evening in Chatteris, a woman became so angry with my alleged March bias that she attacked me with an umbrella, and attempted to shove the tip of her umbrella towards my groin. I might have been completely neutered.

After my free transfer to the *Cambridge Evening News*, Tommy Taylor, the then-manager at the Abbey Stadium, was so unhappy with a match report of a heavy pre-season friendly defeat at Enfield that he threatened to ban me. It would have been some achievement to be barred from attending games before the Football League season even started.

Once I'd joined *The Sun* I gained a different perspective on the issue of perceived bias – because supporters of all clubs think we favour some other club.

Norwich fans probably feel they have always been treated unfairly in the national press, in terms of the amount of coverage. They might not mind minimal column inches when the team is struggling, but when City are doing well, supporters believe the national newspapers do not acknowledge that success sufficiently.

Ultimately, the bigger clubs will always get more coverage simply because of the numbers. But if it is any comfort to my fellow Norwich fans, supporters of Manchester United, Liverpool, Manchester City, Chelsea and Arsenal all feel they are not treated fairly and that we are always too critical.

I disagree strongly with them. In the Premier League, there will always be reasonably-sized previews and reports of games. If one newspaper has an exclusive interview with one of the players, or a big story, then there will obviously be more space given. It's about news priorities, not bias.

As far as Norwich are concerned, the geographic location of the club presents a problem for preview pieces. Because of the cost and the time involved, it is rare for a national newspaper to send a staff reporter to Colney for a routine pre-match press conference with the manager, unless the reporter has an interview lined-up with a player afterwards.

Another factor which affects Norwich coverage is that national newspapers have cut staff levels drastically in recent years. There are fewer reporters than ever. And those who are left must concentrate on the big London clubs and those in Manchester and on Merseyside.

At *The Sun*, we have one reporter covering all the Midlands clubs and only one in the north-east, along with small teams of journalists in the north-west and London. Each reporter has to make a choice when it comes to attending press conferences, because he or she cannot go to all the clubs who have conferences on the same day. So, in the Midlands, the reporter will generally go to Aston Villa rather than Leicester (unless the Leicester manager starts to pick fights with journalists).

There was a time, when Leeds and Sheffield Wednesday were in the Premier League, that all national papers had reporters based in Yorkshire. They were either made redundant or moved into another patch once those teams were relegated.

For clubs in less populous parts of the country, such as East Anglia and the south coast, newspapers rely for their day-to-day team information on agencies or freelance reporters, although most papers (although not all) staff all Premier League games and many in the Championship.

I can tell you, though, that there is certainly no animosity towards Norwich. The majority of national reporters enjoy their trips to Carrow Road. The only complaint over the years has been the length of the journey, but such moans should be rare now that the A11 has been so greatly improved.

The London-based reporters who covered Norwich in the Seventies and Eighties definitely liked going to Carrow Road, perhaps partly because for evening games they were allowed a stop-over at a hotel due to the distance. Now, such luxuries are rare.

Because of the atmosphere and general friendliness, I would suggest few people dislike covering the club. As they enter the media room and smell the food, before giving their name and receiving their accreditation, journalists always turn to look to their left – because that's where the hot food counter is, and the grub at Norwich always smells inviting. I won't name names, but one colleague from London genuinely expected that Delia would be serving the food in the media room. Bless.

Football reporters are not so keen to go to some grounds, whether it is due to location, facilities, the staff who work there or the manager. That latter factor is important because a journalist's experience of working at a football club can depend greatly on the person who sits in the manager's chair and the journalist's relationship – or lack of relationship – with him.

When an experienced coach takes charge of a big club, let's say Louis Van Gaal, you know his attitude will be professional but probably cold. Sometimes, when a new manager is appointed at a club, you have known him as a player or as a manager somewhere else, and that can help. At Norwich, I knew both Glenn Roeder and Bryan Gunn before they took over: Glenn from his time in charge at West Ham and Bryan from his days as a Carrow Road player and his other roles at the club.

As you would expect, the club's former goalkeeping star enjoyed a terrific relationship with all of the media. Glenn's was more fractious. Fortunately, perhaps because I rarely covered Norwich during the worst of his struggles, I got on okay with Glenn. Strangely, Norwich actually did well whenever I went to see his games, and that was something even he clocked. Once, after a post-match press conference, he said, 'Charlie, you are a lucky charm, I should have a picture of you on my keyring.' He was obviously joking. But driving home that evening, I did have a slightly bizarre mental picture of my face being inside one of Glenn's trouser pockets.

Generally, Roeder's relationship with the media could be very strained and the arrival of Gunn was welcomed. That was just a human response of people wanting to work with someone with whom they got on. It is not unusual for many members of the media to be glad when an unpopular manager is fired.

For instance, although they enjoyed the ride at Old Trafford, national media based in the north-west were nevertheless thankful when Alex Ferguson finally left Manchester United, simply because he made the job increasingly difficult. He rarely attended post-match press conferences and refused to allow access to the players. Regardless of how well the team were doing, Ferguson ensured that covering United, although a privilege in many respects, became difficult simply because nobody ever spoke after games.

When Gunn arrived at Norwich, the media were delighted and I think everyone was desperate for him to succeed. Sadly, it was not to be. And so Paul Lambert arrived: the most successful manager in the history of Norwich because of what he achieved in such a short space of time. But Lambert's relationship with the media, particularly the local press, was strained at times. That was unusual because it is often the other way around: managers may not enjoy dealing with the national media but generally have closer relationships with local journos. With Lambert, it was the guys from the nationals who struck up relationships with him. I always found him easy to deal with, even though you needed to be aware that there were two ways of asking the same question.

An occasion which proved that came in a friendly before Lambert's first season in the Premier League in 2011. A national reporter, a good lad but inexperienced, had noted that most of Paul's signings – notably Bradley Johnson, Anthony Pilkington, Elliott Bennett and Steve Morison – had not played top-flight football. It was a fact which could legitimately be put to the manager, and one way to do so would be to ask, 'How confident are you that these inexperienced players can rise to the challenge of playing in the Premier League?'

But, instead, the reporter asked, 'You haven't signed anyone who has played in the Premier so isn't it going to be impossible to keep them up?' Very similar questions, but with a subtle, yet crucial difference. It was the first time Lambert had met this reporter and, needless to say, their relationship started off badly and it was downhill all the way.

Lambert would readily admit that he did not enjoy the camera being pointed in his face or large press conferences. However, I always found him decent value in one-on-one interviews, where he was far more relaxed and had an excellent sense of humour. I remember colleagues from other papers, notably *The Guardian* and *Telegraph*, saying that they were heading to Colney for an exclusive interview with him but they were not particularly looking forward to the experience. On each occasion, those same journalists called me later to say that the Paul Lambert they chatted to for 30 minutes in his office at the training ground was certainly different to the one they had come across after games at Carrow Road.

With the locals, it was all a bit uneasy which is a shame because in his three seasons as boss, there were only good times on the pitch at Norwich, and it ought to have been straightforward off it. At least Paul was consistent, though: he never attempted to hide his disdain for a specific journalist. And actually, I prefer things to be like that than a pretence. I know a few journalists who think they are on excellent terms with certain managers – but those managers are just capable of disguising their feelings during press conferences.

Lambert had to learn to deal with a different situation when he left Norwich for Aston Villa. As I have explained,

national journalists are rarely sent to pre-match press conferences at Colney. There were occasions when the nationals sent
a writer for an interview at a different time, and the nationals
were usually represented at Norwich games, but at pre-match
press conferences, Lambert was mostly dealing with local
media, including agencies and freelances.

On arriving at Villa, the difference for him was that during
every press conference, he was forced to deal with the Midlands
football pack, *en masse*. And when the Midlands Mafia – as they
are known in the business – were not at Villa press conferences,
they would be striving to get Villa stories from other sources.
They would be ringing agents, talking to players, digging for the
latest on a contract or any other news.

I think Lambert adapted and enjoyed an excellent relationship with some of the press although, again, a few were not so
unhappy when he was replaced by Tim Sherwood.

At Norwich, Chris Hughton certainly brought a more laid-
back approach to proceedings. He was a nice bloke, without
actually saying much that was quote-worthy. In some match
reports, even after decent Norwich victories, I included only
about 15 words from Hughton's press conference. Of course,
it was not his job to give the press great quotes for easy head-
lines, his mission was to win football matches, but his cautious
approach in press conferences didn't help him, in my view.

Neil Adams was more in the Gunn camp in terms of
personality. And he had media experience, of course, after
working for Radio Norfolk. Then along came Alex Neil, for
whom the day-to-day experience of managing Norwich compared to Hamilton Accies must have been massively different
– the size of the crowds, the number of journalists he had to
deal with and the facilities at the club.

Certainly, the media facilities at Norwich are now vastly
different from the days when the press were all housed in

the old South Stand – which is where they were when I first covered Norwich. Mind you, I suppose I've changed a bit since then, too, because in those first, professional trips to Norwich, I was working for the *Sunday Sport* and *Daily Sport*.

That came about because, while still working on local papers in the Fens, I took a holiday and had a week working in the *Sport*'s offices in Manchester. To give you an idea what that was like, I was there when the news desk received a call from a woman claiming her son had turned into a fish finger. A reporter was dispatched to her house for the story. The news editor told the reporter to stop at Iceland and buy a pack of Birds Eye fish fingers, as he wanted to stage an identity parade for the woman to pick her son. I kid you not.

Anyway, I got on OK at the *Sport* and started covering football matches at Norwich and Ipswich for them as a freelancer. My 'proper' job was still in March, working on two papers: The *Wisbech Standard* and the *Cambs Times*. I'd do midweek games for my March papers – matches like March v Haverhill, Wisbech Town v Great Yarmouth and Chatteris v Long Sutton – but the paper came out on Friday, so there was no real need to sit and watch matches on the Saturday. Instead, I could ring the relevant manager or club secretary in the week to pick up the facts about their Saturday game. And so I could spend Saturdays working for the *Sport* at Ipswich or Norwich. I didn't work for the *Sport* every Saturday, and when I did my words appeared under a fake name. Some weeks I was Bill London. On other occasions I was Bob Tarpey. They sound like grizzled old London hacks, don't they? But it was the lad from Hunstanton: me.

I was learning my trade but when Norwich qualified for the UEFA Cup, I travelled to the historic first away match, in Arnhem, as a fan. To this day, I still have no idea why I did not take a 40-minute flight from Norwich to Amsterdam followed by a one-hour train to Arnhem. Instead, I drove from March to Carrow Road to catch a club coach that left at midnight.

The journey to Holland was awful. With English teams only recently allowed back into Europe, there was a heavy security and police presence and we were taken to an isolated area in the Dutch city. The Club Canary steward told all of us to be aware of the police dogs. He said, in a broad accent, 'Yoo gotta watch owt. These dogs doont noo the meanun of the werd let goo.'

Of course they didn't. They were Dutch dogs. But I was too tired to laugh.

Because of all the warnings, I was expecting Arnhem to look war-torn and dangerous, yet when we wandered around, it was a lovely place and reminded me of Cambridge. The only danger was that, like Cambridge, you had to watch out for students on bikes.

Due to work commitments (mainly typing up the latest results and tables of the March and District Ladies Darts League) I was unable to go to Munich for Norwich City's most famous European night. But my family was represented at that game by my uncle Paul, a musician who had been based in the Bavarian city since the mid-Seventies.

Immediately after arriving in Munich, he had started supporting Munich 1860, hating their rivals, Bayern, and dreaming of the day, however unlikely, that Norwich would play in Europe. He knew it was fanciful, but he always talked about how wonderful it would be if he could watch Norwich in his new home country.

Not for one moment did he dare to think they might play Bayern, though. That was too far-fetched, even for a dreamer.

Yet, Norwich qualified for Europe, won their first round and then the implausible happened. The draw was made and Norwich were pitted against Bayern. Uncle Paul's German in-laws warned him that his team would suffer a battering.

Lothar Matthäus said pretty much the same. But Germany's most-capped player, and uncle's in-laws were wrong. Little old Norwich became the first – and only – English team to win in Munich's Olympic stadium. And, all these years later, my uncle still cannot believe that night actually happened.

And so to the San Siro. Neil Custis, who is now based in Manchester for *The Sun*, was the *Eastern Daily Press* writer at the game against Inter Milan. By this time, the newspapers I worked for in March were owned by the same group which owned the *EDP*, and so I covered the San Siro game from the terraces for the *EDP*, writing a fan piece – although I paid for my flight. It is incredible when you think that, back in 1993, it cost £300 without a night in a hotel. Now, a family of three can fly to Italy for that.

I remember sitting outside a café when some Norwich fans asked for 'three caffacinos' and another one showing his dismay at being handed an espresso after asking for a coffee. 'I wanted a cup of coffee mate, not a thimble full.'

Norwich should have beaten Inter but, as in the home leg, lost 1-0. They simply did not enjoy the rub of the green. The match was in the afternoon, because it was a public holiday, so when I landed in Norwich there was still time to head back to the office in March and put in a few hours typing out the March Crib League tables.

Because I worked for the group which owned the *Eastern Daily Press* I filled in for Trevor Burton on a couple of occasions to cover Norwich for the paper. That was in 1995 – at home to Manchester City and away to West Ham when the club's relegation fight deepened. That game at Upton Park saw a case of mistaken identity when Andy Johnson was dismissed for an offence committed by Spencer Prior.

Relegation, obviously, hit hard. I was nowhere near the Martin O'Neill era as a journalist because by then I was at the

Cambridge Evening News. But eventually I moved to *The Sun* and I can certainly remember my first Norwich game for the paper, unfortunately. August 9, 1997: Norwich 0, Wolves 2. A 17-year-old Robbie Keane scored twice on his full debut, grabbing a goal in each half.

After that *The Sun* would often give me the games in East Anglia as they knew it was something I enjoyed, whereas the lads who lived in Wimbledon, for instance, preferred covering the likes of Southampton and Portsmouth, which were much nearer.

I was living in Blackheath, in south-east London, but enjoyed heading to East Anglia – until my car developed a problem with the locking system. Basically, it was not working. So, to exit my car, I had to wind down my driver's window and clamber out through the gap. That was OK if I wanted to be outside the car with the window open. If I then wanted to lock the car, I would then have to enter through the boot, climb through the seats and wind the window down before returning to the outside world through the boot and then locking the car.

The locking system was still broken when I had to go to a match at Norwich. I left my home in Blackheath, went to the petrol station and hurdled out through the driver's window – much to the hilarity of a few lorry drivers. Having filled up the car with petrol, and after getting into the vehicle via the boot, I then drove to Norwich and parked at my usual car park on the Lower Clarence Road. I paid, and remember the bemusement of the attendants and a few fans when I climbed through the driver's window, unlocked the boot, climbed over the seats and wound up the driver's window before retreating through the boot – and then heading down the hill towards the media room. It certainly was not a good look.

I covered Norwich's play-off semi-final wins over Wolves in 2002, although I was unable to cover the final against

Birmingham at the Millennium Stadium in Cardiff on May 12, 2002. I had another big match, the day before: my wedding.

Aware that my fiancée was marrying a journalist who might be away for 100 days each year, I decided it would be foolish and disrespectful to disappear to a football game the day after getting hitched. So, I dutifully spent the first day as a married man at our home in Bishop's Stortford, with my wife, playing host to her Italian family.

I did manage to have the game on TV, but the circumstances made watching difficult. And then, at the moment the match went to penalties, the four-year-old daughter of one of my wife's friends wondered about the function of the big button on the front of the TV so she decided to press it. And so, the TV was switched off. By the time I'd turned it on again and it had warmed up, I was greeted by major Birmingham celebrations. That was how I learned Norwich were not heading to the Premier League.

That defeat, though, was not as disappointing as the one at Fulham three years later. Nigel Worthington did well to lead the club to promotion in 2004, but his decision to release Malky Mackay and Iwan Roberts was not one I supported. If Worthington had kept the spine of the team, I think the club would have been clear of relegation without too many problems – and because they went down, I could not see so much of them. Although I continued to watch Norwich as a supporter whenever I could, on Saturdays I was usually somewhere else, because there were not too many chances for me to cover the game for *The Sun* while they remained outside the top-flight.

But, with more of the key Premier League fixtures being staged on Sundays in recent seasons, I've had more Saturdays free for watching Norwich as a punter, although it often means a lot of Saturday night driving.

In the 2014-15 season, following the arrival of Alex Neil

as manager, I got to 17 City games as a fan and took my son to most of them – including both play-off semi-finals against Ipswich. After the decisive Carrow Road leg, I dropped off my son in Bishop's Stortford and then drove 250 miles or so down to Swansea ahead of their home game with Manchester City.

As always, it was a pleasure to see Iwan Roberts who was enthusing about the events 24 hours earlier. I find it intriguing that a number of ex-players not only settle in Norfolk, but become fans of the club. Some supporters may think that former stars do not care. On occasions, this may be true but, equally, there are many players who develop a major bond with a club. Like Iwan and Darren Huckerby at Norwich. Or Ian Wright and Thierry Henry at Arsenal.

Anyway, in the memorable 2014-15 season, I only covered Norwich once for *The Sun*. That was on May 25: the play-off final against Middlesbrough at Wembley. It was a terrific day but also a strange one for me because, as a working journalist, you have to become slightly detached.

The Sun sent three journalists to the game and my task was to write the match report, which, in theory, could have been all about Aitor Karanka, Patrick Bamford and Steve Gibson. I wouldn't have enjoyed writing it, but that was the sort of story a lot of people were expecting and I'd have had to give it my best shot.

Journalists based in the north-east for all the national papers had made the journey down and they arrived with a spring in their step. Not many days earlier they had faced the horrible possibility of not having a single team in the top-flight. Newcastle and Sunderland were both facing relegation while Middlesbrough were by no means guaranteed a promotion spot. That situation was a threat to their jobs because without Premier League teams in an area, there's not a lot of work for national newspaper football hacks.

But Sunderland and Newcastle had survived and Middlesbrough had reached the play-off final so the journalists from the north-east had a jaunty stride at Wembley. They were to leave disappointed – after writing pieces about Neil, Cameron Jerome and Nathan Redmond.

After the match, in 'the mixed zone' – the area where players have to walk past journalists waiting to ask them questions – all the Norwich players were delighted to talk. There were certainly none doing the 'phone trick' of pretending to be speaking to someone so as to avoid talking to the journalists. Yet some of those players will have left Wembley knowing that promotion could signal the end of their Norwich careers. There is very little sentiment about that sort of thing in football.

Nor is there in journalism, a business in which the future is uncertain. People will always want to read about football, there can be no doubt, but with club websites, blogs, free newspapers, 24 hour sports news on TV and updates available on phones, you can only wonder how we will get our football news in a decade, let alone 20 years.

However the news is delivered, there will be some who have the privilege of being paid to cover football and battling to be objective. Being impartial in the press box at a Wembley play-off final is perhaps the hardest test. Trust me on that one.

Charlie Wyett grew up in Hunstanton and began his newspaper career in the Fens before eventually becoming one of the nation's top football reporters as a staff writer on *The Sun*.

5

All Norwich fans can reel off the memorable moments of their City lives. But, for one supporter, those big occasions mostly went horribly wrong.

Jon Rogers, who writes and records songs about the Canaries under the pseudonym Big Grant Holt, tells us about three days which should have been really special but which did not work out as planned.

And, as well as revealing the unlikely musical theme for his sorry saga, he uses his relationship with the game to tell us about another relationship.

ME, MARTINE AND THE STARS

BY JON ROGERS

In case you have forced your brain to remove Martine McCutcheon's fleeting, yet dull singing career, I need to remind you about her 90s single *Perfect Moment*, in which she sang, repeatedly, 'This is my moment, this is my perfect moment with you'. By an unfortunate fluke, it was warbling on my radio just as I was contemplating my own back catalogue of Norwich City moments, and it seemed she was mocking me with her cutting, yet soft tones. The dreary, plod-along of a song just happened to emphasise my inability to grasp vital, transient opportunities in my relationship with the club.

My own Norwich City moments have been anything but perfect. I know fans with tales of vivid, triumphantly rousing highlights of their support for Norwich, but mine are stories of mouldy, ham-fisted failure. Let me explain…

STARS OF THE NIGHT SKY

A few days before my tenth birthday, my dad handed me a letter. A pretty unremarkable letter. White envelope. Rectangular. Might not seem much to you, but when you're that age, ripping opening a letter addressed to you is a rather thrilling few seconds. No banks, bills or bumph, oh no – just competition wins, birthday cards and party invites. It's usually a pretty joyous moment for a-nearly-ten-year-old. This one was amazing. Pulling out and flicking open the paper to its full size, I read:

Dear Jon,

We are pleased to inform you that you have been selected to be the official team mascot for the Norwich City vs. Manchester City game at Carrow Road on Wed 28 August 1991.

Please arrive at the main entrance where we wi… yadda yadda…

My eyes glazed over as the words disappeared into the white of the page, yet the yellow and green Norwich City crest at the peak of the letter still proudly shone. I felt like Charlie Bucket as I had the last golden ticket to the Football Factory.

This was long before the days of having almost as many mascots as players. Back then, there was only one child chosen, and so, for the first time in my young life, I was a singularity. I had uniqueness. I was going to walk out with the players under the floodlights and the night sky at Carrow Road! Wow.

So I did what any other annoying nine-year-old should do at that precise moment: I performed a fake, theatrical faint, and collapsed onto the front room carpet. It can't have been very convincing, because while I was still pretending I couldn't move (yet keeping a tight grasp on the letter), dad presented me another early birthday present: my first full Norwich City kit. The ASICS one. Shirt, shorts and socks. Quite literally the whole kit and caboodle. If I hadn't already been faking a faint, I would have fainted. Three minutes earlier, I had been a school-boy snacking on a banana Munch Bunch yogurt. Now, I had the permission, the uniform and the pressure of being the Official Norwich City Mascot. This was a rather a big deal.

I always had a fascination with the mascots. At every game, I always enviously watched the lucky kid jogging about with the photographer, locating his favourite player, posing for a snap or two and then trotting off towards the goal at the River End to complete a ritual; a task. But this task was the part that both worried and excited me in equal measure.

It was the 1991-92 season. Norwich were in the top division, Division One, back then. In those days, it was customary for the mascot to take a few pot shots at Bryan Gunn. The Scottish goalkeeping legend would save the first two shots but always let the third one in as the River End cheered. It was the tradition of each warm-up. Every mascot did it. And in 48 hours, it would be my turn. What if I missed? What if I punted the ball over the bar and it slapped a fan in the face? What if I chipped it against the post and it bounced back, square into Gunny's groin. How could I live with myself if my fancy attempt put the Norwich Number One out of action? There was only one thing for it: I had to practise.

So for the rest of that day and quite a lot of the evening, while dressed in the full kit, I imagined how it would feel to witness the yellow net ripple. My dad acted the role of Gunn, standing between the school field goalposts. Admittedly, dad didn't have the same physique as Gunny, but he certainly had the same hairline. Yet, with his encouragement, by the end of the long session, I was pinging them in – left, right, top, bottom. I was prepared.

But that didn't stop nerves and excitement pulsing through me on the big day. I became unbearable to live with, and that probably explains why we arrived at the ground really early. As we walked through the main reception, three hours before kick-off, I must have been the only one in the whole football club already in full kit. I looked ridiculous but I didn't care. It was dream-like.

Dad quickly abandoned me with a tremendously tall chap – Dick Chapple, who was tasked with taking me under his wing. He led me away for a quick tour featuring the trophy cabinet, the corridors of power, the manager's and chairman's offices. All very wooden.

As we meandered towards the tunnel to see the pitch for

the first time, the number of personnel present started to grow. It was at this point that I began to experience the ungentlemanly atmosphere of a professional football club. We passed Manchester City players Keith Curle and Niall Quinn, both of whom were swearing vociferously at the various people around them, punctuated with noisy booms of laughter. With wide eyes, I nervously pretended their bad language didn't bother me.

The hubbub grew. People ran around with pieces of paper. Youth players passed me, shaking hands with one another. Other recognisable faces, ones I'd seen in my sticker book or *Shoot* magazine, shuffled about in tracksuits. Suddenly, a programme and a pen were pushed into my hands, and we were off to the dressing room to get each Norwich City player's autograph. Dick, my tall guide and mentor, gave me a warning.

'This is a focused, adult environment, Jon, and you might see and hear things that young men shouldn't hear. Just try not to panic too much,' he said.

Panic? I had just heard Quinny effing and jeffing in the corridor. I used to be a boy, but now? I was down with anything, man. And as for going into the Norwich dressing room, well, I was wearing a proper kit. I was their mascot. I was there for them. I'd spent all those hours taking penalties against my dad in preparation. I was ready.

I was so, so wrong.

As the dressing room doors swung open, I shuffled in and made full eye contact with Ruel Fox's penis. Sharply, I looked away and accidentally clapped eyes on Dale Gordon, half naked on a bench as Tim Sheppard worked roughly on Disco's groin with baby oil. I looked away again, but clapped eyes on the bare bottom of an unidentified player wandering towards the showers. To this day, I still don't know whose backside it was, but it's something I try not to dwell on.

The place was like a dreadful Hall of Mirrors. Bums to the left of me, groins to the right – nowhere was safe. 'A focused, adult environment', Dick had said. 'Try not to panic too much', he had counselled. But everywhere I looked, my innocence was being ripped away from me like cheap wrapping paper at Christmas. Yet a final humiliation was yet to come.

After I had shambled around the room to collect every player's autograph, Dave Phillips told everyone to shut-up while I announced who my favourite player was. 'Er ... Ian ... Ian Butterworth', I trembled. The whole dressing room erupted with laughter as they pointed at Ian in the corner, whose shoulders slumped. I have no idea why they were all so amused. Maybe Mr Butterworth had to pay a fine? Perhaps there was some sort of high level of dressing room gambling going on, 'Who Will The Ugly Kid Choose?' and Butts was in deep. I looked at him apologetically and he rolled eyes in disbelief and turned away from me.

The laughter continued: proper belly laughs which were a lingering roar that didn't stop until the door closed behind me as I was escorted out, holding my match day programme which had been graffitied almost to destruction. Traumatised, exasperated, and failing to gather my thoughts, I looked around for support. Dick put a hand on my shoulder and we waited. In silence. Nobody spoke until the time for me to go stumbling onto the pitch for kick off.

As I mooched out into the floodlit night sky, to roars from the Carrow Road faithful, for my once-in-a-lifetime moment, you might imagine that I thought, 'What a sight! This is the closest I'll ever get to being a footballer! There are 15,376 people staring at you! Lift your head high and breathe that in!"

Not quite. The single thought which filled my mind on this momentous occasion was, 'Wow. Isn't the grass long'. Isn't. The. Grass. Long. I'm ashamed of myself to this day, Martine.

I composed myself to jog off with Mr Photographer for my picture with Ian Butterworth. I stood, all awkward and knobbly knees. He crouched down. I put on my cheesiest grin. He didn't smile. I don't blame him, really, after the dressing room name and shame.

Then, Mr Photographer told me to go towards Bryan Gunn for a few shots.

Oh my goodness! I had totally forgotten about this part. Niall Quinn's profanities, half-naked footballers and the surprisingly long grass had made me blank out my previously lingering fears. But after all my practice, worry and ambition the really big minute had arrived and I was determined not to let myself down.

I took a casual jog over to the River End, where the ball was instantly rolled to me by Gunny, as if he had been waiting for me. I took a touch, set myself and tapped it back. I knew the game. Gunny knew I knew the game, so we danced our merry dance.

He rolled the ball out again. Another gentle shot. He grabbed the ball, bounced it and rolled it out again.

This is my moment. This is my perfect moment with you.

I took a touch. Top left I was going for; I would sweep my laces across the ball. Enjoy it. Breathe it in. Watch this Gunny. Watch this Carrow Road. Watch this world.

'Oi!'

Mark Bowen, who had walked towards me, shouted a gruff warning and gestured belligerently for me to get a move on. His reputation as a grumpy Welshman was obviously justified. I then heard the referee blow hard on his whistle, apparently for the second time. Mr Bowen had a coin to toss and hands to shake, serious Captain business, and I was the one holding up the significant proceedings.

I panicked and turned back to take my shot as quickly as I

could, but Gunny had already jogged off and started his final runs along the eighteen yard box to warm up his long body. I had ruined my chance. The moment had gone. So I never had the opportunity to make the yellow net ripple and, disappointingly, nobody else managed to do so either that night. We drew 0-0. Didn't even win the toss. Not much of a lucky mascot, was I?

STARS IN MY EYES

I was a semi-decent footballer in my youth: very good at a few things, average at most and pitiful at a couple. Like any other normal football-loving kid, I modelled myself on my footballing heroes, who happened to be the stars of the Norwich City squad of the day.

I styled myself on the footballing personas and playing styles of three players: Ian Crook, Darren Eadie and Chris Sutton. It's an eclectic mix, I agree, but if you're thinking of a short, yet dashing smoker, who turned down the England B squad, you've gone completely in the wrong direction.

My passing was based on Crook: pin-point and always aimed to put players 'in behind'. My dribbling skills were copied from Eadie: direct, nippy and daring. My finishing skills were Sutton-eque: swashbuckling yet clinical. (I even nicked his celebration, that 'hooked arm sweep' he used to do with Ruel Fox. Loved that).

To sum up my playing style, I was a typical number ten, operating just behind the main striker, 'in the hole'. But as they didn't really exist when I was little, I think of myself as being ahead of my time. A post-modern footballer, if you will.

Throughout my golden years of playing football, (between the ages of ten and 15) I was regularly turning out for my school during the week, two clubs during the weekend, as well as the bi-weekly PE lesson and, of course, playing outside somewhere until it was too dark, too wet or too cold to do so.

Like most kids my age, I received an array of plastic trophies with little footballers on the top. Quite a few of them marked that I'd been man of the match, some recorded that I was player of the season. One was a top scorer trophy rewarding something like 78 goals. But, if I'm honest, that preposterous number had much to do with the fact that tubby kids not interested in football were frequently made to go in goal at that age, rather than my ability to impersonate Chris Sutton. And although my exploits on the muddy fields of Norfolk were slightly above average, my dream of becoming a professional was about to crash into reality.

The speed bump in the middle of my road to professional football stardom was that as my body grew from boy to man, I had as much mental and physical aggression as Ian Beale on very strong muscle relaxants.

In my early teens – when football became less about 15-7 scorelines and running about in packs and considerably more about; how to spit properly, acquiring the latest boots and kicking the opponent as violently as possible – I proved to be weaker than cheap toilet paper at a wet Glastonbury.

Yet, I still had one opportunity, one moment. My combined Crook, Eadie and Sutton impersonations were decent enough to earn me a trial with Norwich at Trowse. It was nearly October, I was exactly 15 and four weeks old at the time.

On the way there, dad and I drove in mostly silence. I was clearly nervous and I guess dad was too. This was his own version of the golden ticket. If I got signed, I'd be out the house and he'd be set up for life! Pro players were earning nearly ONE thousand pounds a week! A week!! Can you imagine that?

As we pulled into the training ground's car park, he broke our silence with a pep-talk, a poignant father-son moment.

'Everyone here is good, so you need something different to stand out from the crowd. You want to be easy to work with, easy to mould. So, do three things for me. Be respectful, of yourself and others. Be eager; do things you don't want to do. And smile – no-one wants a miserable git. Look like you're enjoying yourself for once.'

The speech penetrated my moody teenage psyche. I'd got it. Be respectful. Be eager. Smile. Easy enough.

Dad handed me a Mars bar, I grabbed my boot bag, left the car and nervously looked for the other triallists. Some chap in shorts told us to get ready in the changing rooms. As I walked into the building at Conley, the strong smell of Deep Heat rolled over me as I found a space, sat on the bench and got changed. There was a nervous quietness. This was it. Start warming those chords, Martine.

Slowly, I took the occasional glimpse up and noticed that all the other footballers seemed to be about a foot wider, two feet taller and three stone heavier than me. One guy looked so mature, I wouldn't have been surprised if his wife and two kids were there to cheer him on. As for the chap on my right, he had stubble that would have made Clint Eastwood proud. I'm even sure I heard a couple of conversations about fixed rate mortgages and which brand of bitter they preferred.

Clint Eastwood decided to make my day. Noticing I was by far the smallest, youngest and most pathetic, he enquired if I knew the whereabouts of the under-eights dressing room. Everyone laughed. He repeated this classic piece of comedy again to each and every boy who hadn't heard. By the seventh time, I wanted to smash his nose in. If I could have reached.

Be respectful.

This allegedly light-hearted bullying would now be classed as 'banter'. Luckily, that horrific term and state of mind didn't exist back then, so I ignored it, sniffed extra hard and made sure my shin pads were on extra tight. Extra, extra tight. The call was given to exit the dressing room, and we all left in single file, our studs crunching in the gravel car park. I caught a glimpse of dad amongst the other parents. He mouthed, 'Good luck'. I quickly mouthed back, 'Get someone to check their bloody birth certificates', nodding towards the giants I was following. We jogged up the small grass mound towards the training pitches where the coach stood. He explained the day, what he expected from us, and lots of other important information – which all washed over me as I was too occupied at the inequality of stature around me. Yet when my name was called out alongside Married Man, Clint Eastwood and the other gangly monsters, the distant hope there had been some admin mix-up on the date, and I had accidentally been invited to an under-20s trial day, quickly disappeared.

The confirmation that these were the guys I was training with did little to settle my nerves. I looked and felt like the final level in a Babushka doll, or Wes Hoolahan's smaller and considerably less talented brother.

Now, at this point, it's important tell you something. I was born on the 30th of August. The penultimate day of the eighth month. That is a big deal in youth football, as it is in education. The start of September is the cut-off date for each year-group. So, if I'd been born a couple of days later, I'd have been in a different school year intake. As it was, I was in the same year-group as lads who had been born the previous September to me.

Got it? No? Well basically, I had JUST turned from 14 to 15. Clint could legally buy cigarettes and light them using a match on his stubble.

You may think that a possible 363 day age-gap is as an excuse as weak as I felt that day, but that gap separated this boy from the men. If my mum and dad had held off for 48 more hours, I'd have been in the younger group of kids at school, and on that pitch at Trowse I'd have been the big lad chatting to the others about mortgage payments, prams or pints. Instead, I was the pipsqueak, there to be battered. But dad's words hit me again. *Be respectful. Be eager. Smile.* I was going to give it my best shot.

The coach asked for forwards. Seven hands shot up, including mine. He laughed and said we'd all have a go but he would need us to play in other positions and take it in turns.

Eager.

I held my hand up higher, as high as it would go. 'I'll play right back', I said. 'I'm a forward but I'll give it a go.' The coach smiled, thanked me, threw me a green bib and made a note on his Canary yellow clipboard of dreams. The other boys saw my eagerness and a couple suddenly decided to volunteer but they didn't get any thanks or any notes jotted down. They just got plonked into other rotten positions. Dad was a genius.

The game kicked off. Two minutes in, the ball floated towards me. First touch, thighed it down. Second touch, brought it out of my feet to the right. Third touch, sent an inward curling, lofted pass into the channel. It dropped just over the opposition full-back's head for the forward to run onto and slot it away. One-nil! A subtle thumbs up from dad and some jotting on the clipboard of dreams.

My fourth touch was a covering clearance for a corner. They attacked, our central defender got done for pace, their striker's touch was heavy but I nipped in, did what all good defenders do – got wiped out, face first into the grass, but cleaned up the danger. Got a clap from the keeper, and another nod from dad.

I had studied enough football to know what the full-back's job was at corners. Basically, you have to camp yourself on the post, bend forward and start playing with your shin pads. Then, bend back up straight and loosely point at someone on the edge of the area. So I did just that, and it worked! A couple of players seemed to shuffle towards the edge of the area where I was pointing, and they even followed when I changed my direction of point! I looked like I knew what I was doing, and had an air of authority about me. Forget Crook, Eadie and Sutton, I was Ian Culverhouse. This playing right-back malarkey was easy.

At that moment, the coach shouted out we only had a few more minutes until we all swapped round positions. Just before the corner came in, I had a few moments to think about dad's pep-talk. He'd said I needed to stand out from the crowd. I thought I'd done that. There were only a few minutes left before I would get my chance to play up top and switch from Culverhouse to Sutton. But for now, I had to stay in character as Culverhouse. Perhaps I would need to perform an overhead kick to clear the ball off the line just to finish my right-back impression off to a tee, but as the corner sailed over, high and looping, Clint Eastwood apparently connected with the ball perfectly first time with his right boot on the six-yard box, and into the goal via a deflection.

I say 'apparently' and 'deflection' as my fifth and very final touch was with my face.

I was told later that the ball hit me at approximately 250 miles per hour. A wallop of a volley, point-blank, smack-bang right in the middle of my nose, which knocked me clean out. The only good thing about being knocked out cold was that I didn't have to witness my teeth violently catapulting away from my mouth. When I was awoken a few seconds later, by an ice-cold sponge on my face, I saw two members of Norwich City youth staff to my left ... and then saw two dads to my right.

Smile. I smiled at both visions of my dad, unsure which one was real and which one brain damage.

As I was driven to A&E to be checked over for concussion I guessed correctly that my professional footballing career was officially over. The biggest impression I had made was with my face onto the leather of the ball. I never got to play up front, I never got another trial.

And as for that stubbled chap who knocked me clean out with his point-blank wonder volley? Mr Eastwood? Do you know who he turned out to be?

I have absolutely no idea, but I hope he's happy for destroying my dream, punk. Still, at least my Norwich career was more successful than Ricky Van Wolfswinkel's, eh?

FALLEN STAR

I don't know if you have heard of it but there was a game Norwich City played versus another team. German I believe, called Bayern Munich. At Carrow Road? In the Nineties?

I am proud to say I witnessed that incredible evening's events. Not all of them, though. If you were at that game, and you saw someone being pulled out by people in luminous orange jackets in the River End – yeah, that was me. Hi.

My dad had bought tickets for the home leg, but for reasons I've failed to comprehend, we had to move from our usual season ticket seats in the safe haven of the family enclosure to the gruff and rough River End. That would be fine in any normal circumstance, or for any normal kid who didn't have the lung capacity of an asthmatic goldfish. (I sound a total drip, don't I?)

Fans used to be able to smoke in the stands in those days and when I say smoke, I mean that it looked like the set of *Stars In Their Eyes* when we walked to our seats. And to cut a long story short, about half way through the second half, the incredible stresses and strains of the pulsating game and the continuous deep breaths of tobacco smoke got to me – I hyperventilated and I semi-fainted onto my dad's arm. This was a real faint, not a thespian response to receiving a letter, might I add.

Yet dad was far too engrossed in the action and noise to realise that his young son, propped up against his arm, had passed out. So I stayed like that until a few moments later, Jerry Goss side-footed the ball into the net. The entire crowd jumped up to roar, as did dad, and I woke with a shock and fell to my knees onto cold damp concrete.

Dad took one look at my pathetically pale face, and the St John's Ambulance volunteers were called. I was brought to my feet, dragged to the corner of the South Stand and River End and dumped in a white-walled first aid room, all shaky and white.

I had missed the equaliser that put Norwich ahead on aggregate. I missed Bryan Gunn having a kerfuffle with Lothar Matthäus. I missed the referee blowing the whistle to confirm our progression to the next round. And when the loudest, proudest On The Ball, City Carrow Road will ever hear rocked the stadium, I was sipping water, shivering next to my dad.

I recall looking up at my dad towards the end of the game, with tears in my eyes, and softly whispering, 'I'm sorry, dad'. He looked down at me, all doe-eyed himself, and I will never forget the simple words he said… 'I should bloody well think so! Bloody missed it all!'

THE STAR IN HIS EYES

So my Norwich's City moments were punctuated with something other than my own inept failure and bouts of unconsciousness. Something much more precious. Or, rather, someone – and I am definitely not talking about Martine this time.

I don't know if you've noticed, but I've mentioned him 26 times. My constant companion throughout the formative years of my love affair with Norwich was my father. Or dad, as I used to call him.

He took me to my first Norwich game. Everton at home. May 1989. Dale Gordon scored late on. 1-0. Dad arranged for that treat of being mascot. September 1991. Then, the next year, he bought me my first season ticket. Our first match: the Sky game v Nottingham Forest, August 1992. People dropped from the sky, there were dancing girls and KWS sung on the pitch. We won 3-1. In 1993, as I was carried out the Bayern Munich match, for over-ventilating, dad was by my side. I could go on and on through each and every year. Until 2011.

The last game we saw, together, was the Portsmouth away game that clinched promotion. It was on telly. He was very ill at this time and mum had propped him up in his chair and pushed it close to the TV. We spent the whole game worrying about him, while he drifted in and out of consciousness, struggling to breathe.

When David Fox's cross was whipped in, and Simeon Jackson nodded it in and sent us back to the Premiership, I was lost in that magical Norwich moment. I jumped up and down, screaming uncontrollably – just like my dad taught me to do, when I saw my first ever Norwich goal back in 1989. I couldn't control myself. But as I shook my arms in the air, my dad sadly couldn't move.

Although, he was a shadow of himself, it's only now I see, *that* was my moment, my perfect moment with him, as not only did that goal save our club, that goal was our last together. A few weeks later, he passed away of lung cancer.

Dad is the reason I am yellow and green, inside and out. It's his fault that I choose the yellow piece in board games. He's responsible for me choosing yellow and green straws in a café. And he is totally culpable for the fact that I shun anything blue and white.

As a hobby, I write original and parody Norwich City songs. The most-watched one so far is called 'Typical Norwich Season'.

They are all on the internet, under the moniker BigGrantHolt – my stage name of sorts. I'm lucky enough to have been in papers, websites, on TV, on radio and to have had the chance to meet lots of charming and loyal Norwich City people. And now I have been invited to write a chapter in this book, I had to fill it with the reason I am who I am, which probably echoes the reasons you are who you are. For every Norwich fan, there is most likely a father, or a mother, or aunt, uncle, big brother, whoever…to blame for that yellow and green infection inside us that brings us joy, despair and every repulsive and magnificent emotion in between.

Dad's passing left a big hole in my life, and the time and efforts I put into BigGrantHolt projects are an attempt to fill that gap. In a way, his death accidentally brought such a positive new chapter of my life but, of course, he had no idea of it all. He never heard a single note of my songs or will ever read a single syllable of the words I write, but I believe he would have treasured everything I've done and been immensely proud.

I still try and follow his words everyday. *Be respectful. Be eager. Smile.* It's such good advice for anything you do in life, and if he could have a couple minutes just to come back say a few more words, I'm sure he would look me in the eyes, and say, 'Sorry, son'.

And I'd simply reply, 'I should bloody well think so! You've missed it all!'

Carrow Road season-ticket holder **Jon Rogers** is better known as BigGrantHolt, the pseudonym he uses on YouTube, where his songs about Norwich City have given him cult status. All together now: 'Jamie Cureton's green hair, Russell Martin's underwear, Ruel Fox, Jerry Goss…'

6

And now for something completely different: a scholarly, nay educational, study of the evolution of the Norwich City mascot, Captain Canary.

Lilie Ferrari has traced the Captain's ancestry – from a moon-faced dumpling via a beauty queen – and by doing so gives a social history of our football club.

She interviewed Splat the Cat and learned about the Lemur but leaves us with a mystery involving the Captain's girlfriend, Camilla Canary.

O CAPTAIN! MY CAPTAIN

BY LILIE FERRARI

I have spent a large part of my life writing soap operas, so it will come as no surprise when I reveal that during the many hours passed at Carrow Road, I have spent the leaner moments (you know what they are) musing on the scenario for Carrow Road – The Soap.

This is how it goes: Delia Smith and Michael Wynn Jones are the long-suffering parents, the matriarch and patriarch of this particular soap world. Alex Neil is the hard-grafting older son, ambitious, determined, a leader of men. He has a lot of foster brothers – erm – shall we say numbering somewhere between eleven and, say, forty-one? They're a mixed bunch. Some are wayward, badly behaved, hell-raising in nightclubs, shacking up with unsuitable partners, but inevitably, as is the way with continuing dramas, they don't last long. Others are handsome and virile, fit and strong, eager to succeed, and last longer in the unfolding story that is NCFC. There's also the Big Boss, David McNally, who runs the all-powerful Canary Football Factory, where our band of brothers must work to survive. So far, so grim and gritty. But what about light relief? It's often supplied in soaps by stories about characters' pets – dogs go missing, cats get kidnapped, snakes escape – all fun stuff to leaven all that soap despair.

So what does our soap have? Well. You know the answer to that: our very own Captain Canary, a bird (albeit a rather large one) following in the honourable tradition of soap. *Coronation*

Street had Mavis's budgies and Jack Duckworth's pigeons. *EastEnders* briefly had a parrot, several lovebirds and a budgie called Joey, owned by Dot Cotton and accidentally vacuumed up by Jim Branning. So the Captain fits nicely into the on-going story of Carrow Road. He's always there, flitting around the touchline before the game, posing for photos, dancing, waving, high-fiving young fans. He even has his own page in the programme. But who is the real Captain Canary? Why is he here? Where does he come from? What is the story of his past? It's been a long time coming, but here it is – the story of the Captain, his cohorts past and present, and his origins.

According to the Oxford English dictionary, the word 'mascot' comes from France – the gorgeous region of Provence, to be exact, basking by the Mediterranean. They used a word *mascotto* to describe anything that brought luck to a household, derived from the word *masco*, meaning a witch. But before the word entered our language, some British Army regiments had real animals as good luck charms of a sort. During the Indian Mutiny Campaign of the 1850s, the 95th Derbyshire Foot Regiment adopted a ram as a talisman, and that animal later became a symbol associated with the city of Derby – and of course then Derby County FC, still known as 'the Rams'.

By the early 1900s football in the UK was swamped with mascots of the live variety: Newcastle had a Great Dane, Manchester United paraded a billy-goat round the pitch, and Sheffield Wednesday had their own monkey, resplendent with blue and white ribbons. According to *Soccer History* (1), this practice of adopting animal mascots faded when football resumed after the First World War, and human-beings began to appear on the nation's pitches dressed in costumes – something that continued well into the 1950s. These were usually supporters wearing home-made fancy-dress outfits who paraded outside grounds and posed for press photographers. These early mascots were there to entertain the fans, encouraging the singing of club songs and interacting with home and away supporters. They became increasingly prominent, and were sometimes permitted to walk around the perimeter of the pitch before matches, as pictorial evidence shows they were during Norwich City's cup run in 1959.

Indeed Norwich City had several unofficial mascots, including Peter Cooper, who had attended each of City's matches home and away for five seasons until November 1966, when he had to go into hospital and missed several fixtures. The fact that this was noted in the press is evidence of how important mascots had become. Peter Cooper accompanied the team on to the pitch in an era when there was none of the fanfare accompanying our current players at the start of the game – and so his absence was noteworthy.

Another mascot, Peter Judd, featured in the Football League Review of 1965, having been a mascot for fifteen years. 'I go around with my umbrella and rattle to get crowds into a good humour,' he said. 'I love to settle a Norwich balloon on the centre circle and then get the local lads to run out and pop it.' There was also Bert 'Nobby' Clarke, another star of the '59 cup run. About five feet tall, he was rumoured to have been a circus performer as a boy, and as an adult was a well-known ferryman taking people across the Yare to Whitlingham in the 1940s and 1950s. He used to take football supporters down to Carrow Road where, like the aforementioned Peters, Cooper and Judd, he was an unofficial mascot. He would also appear at events on the river on his water cycle (which was called Nutty Slack) dressed in his trademark yellow and green.

The rise of hooliganism in the mid-1960s meant that interaction with the crowd was not such a good idea. Unofficial mascots began to fade away. The new watchwords, inspired by the 1966 World Cup, were marketing and promotion, and heralded the arrival of World Cup Willie, the FA's official mascot, described as 'a lion with a Beatle haircut, a Union Jack jersey and an address somewhere in Yogi Bear's Jellystone Park'. This commercial venture, based on the sale of football-related World Cup Willie toys, clothes and even beer, was a massive success for the FA. This ubiquitous mascot (who even had a hit record sung by Lonnie Donegan) inspired British clubs to rethink their marketing strategies, and two clubs employed Walter Tuckwell and Associates – the firm that had devised World Cup Willie – to create mascots for their clubs. Beau Brummie materialised to support the 'Rebirth of the Blues' campaign launched in 1966 by Birmingham City, and the following January, Ozzie Owl arrived for Sheffield Wednesday's centenary. But these figures were not mascots as we know them. At best, they were cardboard cut-outs that decorated the clubs' shop windows; but generally they were cartoon figures that adorned all manner of marketable items from pencils to T-shirts. They were the forerunners of the myriad of furry hulks that stumble around our grounds today, but it wasn't until the 1980s that the trend towards giant creatures representing clubs began.

It's interesting to note that in the Sexist Seventies (as I like to call them), the Canaries ran out onto the pitch accompanied by a young woman wearing, according to one observer, a kit several sizes too small for her. There's a photo in Canary Citizens (2) of a certain June Stangroom, a 21-year-old assistant salesgirl from New Costessey, giving the camera 'a first Division smile after being voted Miss Canary 1972.' She was, apparently, Norwich City's first-ever Division One beauty queen, having been voted in at the Supporters' Social Club, winning the title from an entry of ten. Where are you now, June Stangroom? – And did you have successors? No-one seems to know, but in a flurry of realisation that some supporters aren't men, the late Seventies and early Eighties also saw the arrival of short-skirted or short-shorted cheerleaders onto the touchline before matches and at half time. No, I'm wrong, of course. The flurry of realisation was probably that the majority of supporters at the time were men, and might possibly appreciate a babe or two on the pitch. Or not: the fad didn't seem to last long. My memory of those cheerleaders is of some embarrassed-looking girls from a local dance academy waving their green and yellow pompoms in a disorderly fashion and doing a little bit of jumping around. Having attended football games in the States, I think I can safely say that we never quite reached the showbiz pizzazz of the Dallas Cowgirls and their ilk...

It was at City's game against Stoke in the 1980-81 season that Carrow Road saw the first appearance of two very official mascots: Canary and Dumpling. A photograph from the time shows the elegant, tall figure of Canary, every inch the gentleman in yellow and green windowpane check trousers, a black tailcoat and waistcoat, yellow bow tie and top hat, white gloves and spats, carrying a gold-topped cane. Under the top hat is a perky-looking, large-beaked canary head which somehow gives the impression of old-school aristocracy – which fits with the idea of the time, apparently, that Canary would represent the relative sophistication of the City, while Dumpling was the living (?) embodiment of rural fans (how to divide your supporters in one great big marketing faux pas...).

Dumpling, I am sorry to say, was a moon-faced, grinning pudding-head wearing a green and yellow porkpie hat, a farmer's smock and an NCFC rosette. City triumphed in the game, beating Stoke 5-1, including a Justin Fashanu hat trick – so here was the first evidence that our official mascots might in fact bring the team luck. However, in the photograph, a very indifferent-looking Roger Hansbury is brushing past the mascots without a backward glance, followed by two late and great but equally preoccupied players, Graham Paddon and Fash himself. So is it possible that even at that early stage the players did not share the crowd's enthusiasm for talismen...?

Canary and Dumpling were born in a small studio room in the back of a terrace house in Wood Street, Norwich. Their creator was Edgar Henry Banger, known as Harry Banger, born in 1897, a cartoonist whose work featured in popular comics of the 1930s, and whose most famous illustrated off-spring was Koko the Pup for DC Thompson's Magic comic. In Norfolk, Harry was a well-loved regular cartoonist for local papers like the *Eastern Daily Press*, the *Eastern Evening News* and *The Pink 'Un*, in which cartoon versions of Canary and Dumpling often featured. Sadly, Harry Banger never got to see his creations made flesh on the pitch: he died in 1968, some twelve years prior to the mascots' first appearance at Carrow Road.

The football website *No Standing (A trip down the Corridor of Uncertainty)* describes the pairing of Canary and Dumpling as 'weird and somewhat scary'. It reports that 'the over-sized dumpling head and sharp-beaked canary in full evening dress looked like characters from a German fairy tale, guaranteed to give young supporters nightmares! They also elicited howls of derision from away fans. No wonder Norwich City 'retired' the mascots and consigned them to the Bridewell Museum...'

Why a Canary? And – even more puzzling now – why a Dumpling? The football mascots may have represented inner city style and rural vulgarity to their Carrow Road creators, but cartoonist and originator Harry Banger was harking back to early Norwich history for the Canary, and to a local culinary speciality for the Dumpling. Canaries arrived in Norwich with the influx of the 'strangers' in the 17th century, asylum seekers from the Low Countries fleeing religious persecution, who brought their weaving and dyeing skills to the City along with their favourite singing birds in little wooden cages –

canaries originating from the Dutch colonies in the Caribbean. The Flemish weavers were so successful and so resented that there were UKIP-style demonstrations in Norwich, with locals complaining the incomers had pinched their jobs ('twas ever thus…). Strange, then, that the birds these interlopers loved so much should become an emblem of the city they adopted.

The yellow and green canary colours didn't start with the birth of football in the city. Originally the club was known as the Citizens ('Cits' for short), players wore blue and white striped shirts (horrors!) and played on a sports field on New-market Road, still in use today by Town Close House School.

The first mention of that small yellow bird in connection with the club came in 1905, when a young secretary/manager from Queens Park Rangers was selected to run Norwich City FC. The Canary Citizens (3) quotes from this fulsome description of the new manager in the *Eastern Daily Press*: 'Frankness seems stamped upon his agreeable features….Not every man glows with enthusiasm when the topic of conversation turns upon his daily work, but as the light kindles in John Bowman's bright grey eyes, it is easy to see that he loves the game and the sport…His forehead, from which the dark hair is brushed upwards, seems to indicate the brainy, intelligent player who makes for the good of the game.'

At the end of his first season, Bowman's team were at the top of the Norfolk and Suffolk League and were later elected to the dizzy heights of the Southern League. At the youthful age of 26 when he arrived in Norwich to take over, there are some tempting parallels to draw with the profile of our current manager – apart from the hair, of course. Bowman, in his initial interview with the *EDP*, was asked if he knew anything about Norwich, to which he replied, 'I knew of the City's existence…. and I have since heard of the canaries.'

And so the Canaries as a football team, were born – although

Wikipedia offers a different explanation: ' In 1907…. the club's chairman (who was a keen breeder of canaries) dubbed his boys 'The Canaries' and changed their strip to yellow and green'.

Hmm. You pays your money and you takes your choice… But whatever the true origin, the naming of the team as the Canaries over a hundred years ago begat our evolving procession of Canary mascots, from that first Canary who suavely accompanied the Dumpling round the pitch, to our current Captain, of whom more later.

On to that grinning, pudding-faced companion. *Information Britain* (4) describes Norfolk dumplings as 'intended to fill hungry stomachs cheaply so that the paucity of the meat course was less noticeable. Unlike Yorkshire Puddings, however, they have always been served with the meat, rather than before it.' Guest house landladies in the popular Norfolk holiday resorts served these dumplings to their guests to reduce costs, and so the fame of the Norfolk dumpling was disseminated throughout the land. Unlike other dumplings, a Norfolk dumpling is made from bread dough, containing no suet, and should rise to the top of whatever it's cooked in (sorry, Delia – this isn't my territory…) – hence the Norfolk names for them - floaters or swimmers. Suet dumplings, on the other hand are known as sinkers in Norfolk, for obvious reasons. I feel I should add a sentence or two here about other, more lavatorial meanings for these words, but that would require an entirely different article for an entirely different publication (possibly one entitled *Loophemisms*…).

Norfolk people came to be known as 'Norfolk Dumplings' in the same way that Yorkshire folk are called 'Tykes' (a dialect word for a Yorkshire terrier) and residents of Ipswich are known as, among other things, 'Tractor Boys'. (I am employing what is known as journalistic restraint here…) And thus it was in the beginning that the canary and the dumpling became the representatives, whether we like it or not, of our county and our football club. David Cuffley told the *Evening News* (5) how he and a colleague borrowed the Canary and Dumpling costumes for a fifth round FA Cup game at Derby in 1984. 'We went out on the pitch before kick off and I was glad I was wearing a big fibreglass dumpling head as various missiles bounced off as we went past the Derby fans. The Derby mascot was a live ram getting under our feet... a little bit lively.' No-one said it was easy being a Dumpling.

By the mid 1990s, the club's head of marketing Andy Cullen (now selling up a storm at MK Dons) began to see the need to attract younger supporters to the game. For me there are interesting parallels here with the business of television. Many times I have been told by TV management that the audience is middle-aged and static and that we need to find a way to encourage new, young, loyal viewers. The same is true of football supporters. On August 23rd 1995, 'Family Night Football' made its first appearance at Carrow Road: a combination of entertainment ideas to attract children to City's reserve matches. There was a clown called Razz, face-painting, balloon animals and the like, all happening in the Barclay Stand. Although no-one will actually confirm it, personnel at the club seem jointly convinced that this was the date, year and time when the first Captain Canary put in an appearance. The game, incidentally was a 6-0 triumph for the reserves against Swindon Town, with Mike Sheron scoring a hat-trick. Could a pattern be developing here...?

The original Captain had what Aunt Erica, a columnist in the matchday programme, describes as 'the fixed stare of a deranged psychopath'. He also had a cloak. Rumour has it that the idea came directly from chairman Robert Chase – to flatter the superheroes of comic book fame by emulating them with our own yellow and green cloak-wearing nemesis. Captain

Marvel, Captain America – why not Captain Canary? (You don't have to answer that…) The only other canary hero in existence is in DC Comic's *Arrow* series, and she's an ultra-shapely young woman called Black Canary, so clearly no relation.

A study of photographs of Captain Canary at the time shows a sad-eyed, heavy-lidded bird with manicured eyebrows and a slightly sagging beak. He's wearing satin shorts and a vest with two intertwining C's on a green shield adorning the chest area (astonishingly, there is no record of Coco Chanel suing the club for breach of trademark), and a green satin cape sagging limply round those giant shoulders. With his rotund yellow body atop a pair of gargantuan feet, Captain Canary was a far cry from his elegant, evening-suited cane-carrying ancestor. To quote one philosophical supporter who wishes to remain anonymous: 'The Captain's costume allowed him to do little more than waddle about and wave at people. And we all know that doesn't get one very far in life…' (He has obviously forgotten about the Queen Mother.)

By August 1998 Erica Halfhold-Nelson (to give her full name) was writing in the programme: 'Our own Captain Canary has obviously benefitted from the new fitness regime at the Club. He no longer resembles his predecessor, Dumpling, but has been transformed into a slim, lithe figure like, well, Iwan Roberts. He is sprightly when once he was only able to waddle a few yards before munching greedily on a great slab of Delia's seed cake… The depressed, beady stare, akin to Neil Adams' after a particularly bad refereeing decision, has been replaced by a mischievous grin. He no longer has to tug nervously at his shorts which fail to encompass his ample waistline. He has come to accept that the cape is no longer a plausible fashion accessory.'

Thus we arrive at the current incarnation of the Captain, although the date of the first appearance of his female

partner, Camilla Canary, is unclear. She certainly features in
Rick Minter's book *Mascots: Football's Furry Friends* (6) in all her
eyelashed, fluffy-hatted glory, one arm round a young fan while
at the same time employing her other yellow satin-gloved hand
to swig a bottle of champagne. She may already have been
present when Family Night Football was rebranded as
'Soccer PM', again in a strategy to inspire and retain the
loyalty of young fans at reserve games, there being little doubt
that Camilla was introduced to attract young female fans to the
game. At the time of the *Mascots'* publication, there were no
fewer than 15 male and female 'couple' mascots, although as
with our own club, that number has dwindled since. In Minter's
book, the Captain describes Camilla as his girlfriend, and
that is what she remained – no wedding ever took place at
Carrow Road between the lovebirds, as it did between Aston
Villa's Hercules and Bella in 2000 – an event of such importance
it even featured on *Match of the Day*.

The departure of Camilla is as shrouded in mystery as her
arrival, and questions to club officials regarding her fate have
met with obfuscation, and so I am obliged to leave her current
whereabouts to your imagination – or a very funny online
Holtamaniablog which reproduces a largely unrepeatable Captain
Canary's diary entry for August 2011 as follows: 'Dear Diary,
today I went to walk in the rain but I still couldn't feel anything.
They said it would help, but nothing does. Nothing ever helps.
It's been three long years since she walked out and I think about
her every day. All I got was a letter stuck to the fridge. Now I
keep it in my wallet. I'm talking about Camilla of course. We
were perfect for each other...'

After a controversial imagining of the Captain's day, the
entry concludes: 'But it's all in the past. She's gone and now
it's me drinking Super Tennents in the day, in my office. I lock
the door so Splat can't get in. He tells me I need to move on,

but what does he know? ... He isn't going to bring her back, he isn't going to replace the void that she left behind. I don't know where to go from here. It all feels just meaningless, like the Johnstone's Paint Trophy. When I stand in the rain it looks like I'm crying, but I'm not.'

This was a sponsor-rich period in the club's history, involving at one time a giant mobile phone that always seemed to have trouble bowing its head in a respectful way during one-minute silences on the pitch. One of the Captain and Camilla's longest-serving companions was the eponymous Splat the Cat. Aaaah, Splat – he of the blue and yellow striped fur, Pluto-sized head and manic grin. Sponsored by the Norwich and Peterborough Building Society, he first appeared at a reserves' 5-1 defeat at home to West Ham – so much for the pattern established by the debut appearances of his canary companions. Yet Splat was, according to one supporter, 'extremely popular. He was agile, springy and displayed a sense of visual humour. Most importantly his inner self seemed entirely at one with the role.' (Seriously. He actually said that. I wrote it down in my notebook.) Aunt Erica described the trio thus: 'A curiously exaggerated bird skips about the corridors of power fluttering her eyelashes at admirers and tugging up her frilly shorts in defiance of detractors. Flanking her, doleful and ponderous, strides a barrel-chested canary with a cranium the size of a coal skuttle, and a seven foot tall yellow and blue cat…'

I was fortunate enough to conduct a telephone interview with Splat, now retired. This was a real coup, as normally mascots are completely silent; and of course I'm still not entirely sure it was Splat I spoke to, but I was given his phone number by someone at the club, so I can only hope... Splat was clearly a cat who relished his role on the pitch. Memories of his time at Carrow Road were vivid and plentiful. He was proud to have instigated a pre-match ritual involving Iwan Roberts, which is confirmed by the great man himself in his autobiography *All I want for Christmas* (7). Splat told me that Iwan always bent down to tie his shoelaces before each match, and while he was thus employed, Splat came along and ruffled his hair. This resulted in a win for the club, and so Splat began his own good luck pantomime, performed at every game, described by Iwan: 'Our mascot, Splat the Cat, annoys me because his superstition is coming up to me as I'm bent over and ruffling my hair. Sod off! It's taken me half an hour to get it looking that good!'

Splat revealed to me that he has a twin – another blue and yellow cat (obvs) at Peterborough United FC, which should come as no surprise (but does), given the sponsors. City Splat assured me that they weren't identical, claiming that he was more agile than his Posh counterpart, who retired earlier.

Our blue and yellow cat did duty home and away for nine years, and occasionally tangled with the stars, including one memorable Manchester United game at Carrow Road in 2005, when at half time he kicked the ball at substitute Wayne Rooney warming up on the pitch, and shouted 'nuts!'. Cristiano Ronaldo then attempted to hit Splat with the ball, but missed, occasioning some joshing from our feline friend. I need hardly add that we won 2-0, in spite of both Ronaldo and Rooney coming on in the second half. In fact Rooney, obviously still miffed, was booked for a foul on Helveg in the 54th minute.

On another occasion, Splat recalled, he followed Gordon Bennett round the pitch twirling a giant pair of specs and carrying a large clipboard, in imitation of the Chief Executive, who twirled his own specs and had a smaller clipboard, and who loved it. Sadly, this little comedy routine earned Splat a reprimand, as did another incident, when he was performing PR duties at a charity event, forgot himself for a moment and (children turn away now) removed his head. Small wonder that Splat's nine lives eventually ran out in 2008, in spite of his ebullient personality. It even occasioned a debate on a *Pink 'Un* web forum about whether Splat was superior to Captain Canary, which Splat won (by a whisker, of course), one contributor posting, 'My vote goes to Splat the Cat, for away fan and ground staff baiting...' although someone called Sports Desk Pete writes mysteriously, 'My vote goes to the Colman's pig (sadly missed)...' The Colman's pig...?! Must have been a brief appearance, and before my time...

It always seemed to me that putting a cat and a canary on the same pitch was asking for trouble. But in spite of the many antics of other mascots around the country, Splat and the Captain politely kept their distance and their dignity. The punch-up between Wolfie of Wolves and all three of Bristol City's pigs has gone down in mascot history, as has that most notorious mascot bad boy Cyril the Swan, who was once handed a £1,000 fine for a solo pitch invasion and on another occasion ripped the head off Millwall's Zampa the Lion and drop-kicked it into the crowd, as BBC Sport Online's Neil Hall recounted in a 2001 website piece entitled *When Mascots go Bad*.

Sadly, Captain Canary, while avoiding negative controversy, has not exactly covered himself in glory either. He has never won the Mascot Grand National since its inauguration in 1999. Starting at Huntingdon and later moving to Kempton Race Course, the race now seems to have lapsed, with no record of it having taken place in 2014 or 2015, possibly due to recent scandals involving trained athletes replacing the real mascot runners in order to win for their club.

However there is another race, the Sue Ryder Mascot Gold Cup at Wetherby, recently won by Ronnie Rhino, representative of Leeds Rhinos (rugby), and this year accompanied by a heartening announcement for all feminist mascot fans: 'After careful consideration of the nominations, our judges have decided that the JCT600 sponsored UK Mascot of the

Year for 2015 is Berry Bear of the FA Group. Berry works tirelessly to help promote women and girls' football in England. As this year is The FIFA Women's World Cup, Berry is doing her utmost to encourage families to get involved in football and support the Lionesses in Canada in June.'

Captain Canary does not appear to have participated in the Gold Cup, but I urge all right-thinking people to go online and look at the footage of earlier races, even if they show the Captain in a poor light. There's some fine footage of the 2004 Grand National which clearly reveals Captain Canary stumbling along somewhere among the back runners and not even attempting the jumps, while a winning Graham the Gorilla (Finedon Volta FC) triumphantly sprints past the post.

Splat's appearances in Norwich did overlap briefly with the brainchild of ten-year-old competition winner Steven Fackman – the Aviva Lemur, a goggle-eyed creature in City kit currently circling the pitch with the Captain, and the most recent addition to that strange phalanx of mascots who have irritated us, made us laugh, geed up the kids before kick-off, baited the away fans and generally aroused either massive emotion or complete indifference amongst City supporters. And mention must be made of the child mascots (five to 14 year olds) who accompany the players onto the pitch these days (the tallest child always somehow mischievously paired up with Wes Hoolahan). These children pay for the privilege of posing with their heroes, although one child at every match who is considered a deserving case goes free – and they are all clearly in football heaven as they run out onto the hallowed turf at Carrow Road, to the delight of doting relatives.

To bring the mascot story right up to date, the *Evening News* recently ran a story about their former sports writer David Cuffley who was joined by 63 other football fans on the pitch at Wembley to sing Abide with Me prior to the 2015 FA Cup

Final, proudly wearing his Norwich City shirt. How did he win this honour? – By penning a piece, already mentioned here, about the time in 1984 when he wore the Dumpling's head and got chased by the Derby Ram...

So there we have it: furry club mascots like Captain Canary; children appearing as match day mascots; official, sponsored mascots like Splat and the Aviva Lemur, and unofficial, impromptu mascots, from Nobby Clarke on his water cycle to our current Canary Fairy, a burly bloke patrolling the stands in a green and yellow tutu.

Luck plays an enormous part in the game that is football, and the superstitions and rituals that accompany it, embodied in the mascot, are as powerful for some as the game itself. Roger Munby, erstwhile chairman, once wisely remarked that football is 'theatre with an unpredictable outcome'. It's that absolute unpredictability that induces fans to try and meddle with fate. Supporters wear lucky charms and badges, own pendants, flags and toy animals in club colours, and some adopt the 'lucky underpants' habit that even players admit to (Iwan Roberts again).

Football is show business. It's family entertainment, even if some members of the Snakepit would disagree. It matters, of course, in all sorts of ways, to communities, to counties, towns and cities, and even forms a part of our national identity. As well as being sport, it's also recreation – and recreation involves fun. So sneer at our barrel-chested, huge-headed furry mammoths stumbling round the touchline if you will; I prefer to see them as a funny and integral part of the magnificent ongoing soap opera that is Norwich City Football Club. Long may they – and it – continue!

Lilie Ferrari is a novelist and script-writer. She was a script editor of EastEnders and has written episodes of many popular television series and dramas. Oh, and she's a mad keen City supporter and Carrow Road regular.

Acknowledgements

With thanks to Phil Gray, Erica Halfhold-Nelson, Karen Buchanan, and other City supporters who prefer to remain anonymous.

Notes

1. www.soccer-history.co.uk Issue 20
2. *Canary Citizens Centenary Edition* by Mike Davage, John Eastwood, Kevan Platt. Jarrold Publishing 2002
3. Ibid
4. www.information-britain.co.uk
5. David's Derby dumpling adventure …Kim Briscoe, *Evening News* April 22, 2015
6. *Mascots: Football's Furry Friends* by Rick Minter. Tempus Publishing Ltd 2004
7. *All I want for Christmas…* by Iwan Roberts with Karen Buchanan. Vision Sports Publishing 2004

As a boy, he received a dodgy football present, but **Simon Thomas** has strived hard not to be a dodgy football presenter, even when faced with the ultimate test of his professional impartiality: fronting national television coverage of the biggest East Anglian derbies of all time – and then finding himself 'ringside' at Wembley.

This is the engaging tale of how a former *Blue Peter* star became a Yellow, and how a Carrow Road shocker helped him reach for the Sky.

THAT GOAL, THE WRONG SHIRT
AND A LATE PARTY

BY SIMON THOMAS

It was 1:59pm on a certain Monday afternoon in May 2015. I stood in a suit with a microphone in hand on the Wembley touchline, surveying green and yellow adorned fans pouring into the stadium. I looked ten rows back to where my sister and family were sat. I saw their faces full of excitement and anticipation and I felt a wave of emotion. But the voice from TV gallery in my ear told me, 'On air in 10, 9, 8, 7...' It was time to flick the switch in my mind to professional mode and attempt to play the next four hours with the straightest of bats.

But what that magic Monday did do, more than anything else, was remind me why I'm so glad that 36 years before I had decided to follow my heart and not the crowd.

THAT GOAL

It was 1979 and Bob Paisley's Liverpool were in their pomp, sweeping away everything that stood between them and their 11th League title. The year before, with Hughes, Hansen, Clemence and Souness in their ranks, they had won the second of their five European crowns at Wembley Stadium as the irrepressible Kenny Dalglish scored the only goal. They were a team of heroes; they were *the* team to beat; they were *the* team to follow.

And in the village of Grimston in West Norfolk, where I grew up, their red shirts dominated the pitch at football practice. The yellow and green of a club 33 miles away barely got a look in.

It was the same in playgrounds and gardens. My best friend Mark Howlett always wanted to be either Ian Rush or Kenny Dalglish, for instance – and to this day I can't explain why I didn't jump on the Liverpool bandwagon. I could pretend that, even at the age of six, I had decided that a true football fan should always follow his local team, but that would be a lie. But, on 9 February, 1980, an 18-year-old called Justin Fashanu lit up Carrow Road and my football passion and loyalty were confirmed forever.

Although *that* goal was scored on a pitch that bore a passing resemblance to a ploughed field next to the A47, the build-up was the sort of football the opposing Liverpool team delivered week-in week-out. The finish wasn't. The men in yellow and green neatly shifted the ball from left to right before it arrived at the feet of John Ryan. Ryan's lovely first time pass forward took Ray Kennedy out of the equation and found the feet of Fashanu…

I was sitting in the lounge with my old man watching *Match of the Day* transfixed as, in one poetic move, the young striker, undeterred by the attentions of left back Alan Kennedy, flicked the ball up and away from his marker with his right foot before unleashing the sweetest of volleys with his left, past Ray Clemence, leaving the brilliant Barry Davies screaming, 'Oh what a goal. Oh that's a magnificent goal'. It was the magical moment for me when it all clicked. I had a hero and he wore the green and yellow of a team who were now, indisputably, my team.

The football world my son, Ethan, is growing up in today is unrecognisable from the one I grew up in. Mine was a time when, in comparison to today, there was very little football on the box and so moments like Fashanu's at Carrow Road felt incredibly special.

This is not the place to recount how Justin Fashanu's life unfolded after that goal, but there is one episode that cemented him as one of my Canary heroes for evermore. As a 'man of the cloth', my dad recorded a series of 'Thoughts for the Day' for BBC Radio Norfolk and a few weeks after that goal, on his way out of the then Surrey Street studios, he bumped into the Norwich City number nine.

A few hours later, back in Grimston, I arrived home from school to be greeted by the old man with a grin on his face as wide as the River Wensum. He was holding a small piece of green paper. 'I've got something rather special for you' he said, and handed me the paper. On it were the words, 'Dear Simon, With Best Wishes, Justin Fashanu'.

Now that I have signed the occasional autograph myself, I know this is the standard formula, but to a seven-year-old kid it meant everything and then some. Justin Fashanu, the player I attempted to emulate in my garden with my cheap garage-forecourt football, had written a note especially for me! In many ways this was the moment football, and what it was to follow a club, became real. Until this point it had all felt a bit abstract. I knew about the game. I knew about Norwich and had seen them on television a bit. But it wasn't much more than this.

The small piece of green paper was pinned carefully to the top right-hand corner of my bedroom notice board where it remained throughout my school days, as we moved from Norfolk down to Surrey, and later on to Suffolk. Many years later, after I heard of Fashanu's death, I was back at my parents' house in Beccles and had a dig around in the garage. Among the boxes and dusty artefacts of my youth was the cork notice-board with the small green piece of paper displaying Justin's words in faded blue biro.

THE WRONG SHIRT

As I say, my local football practice was awash with Liverpool shirts. There were yellow shirts – because that was the colour of Liverpool's away kit. To wear a Norwich kit meant you were the odd one out. Or odd two. There were a couple of brave young souls. This wouldn't have deterred me. I would have proudly worn one too but my dad, on a vicar's salary, found that a 'proper' kit was a bit of a stretch. For some months I had to make do with a Debenhams mash-up of plain navy shorts and a black top. But then something rather disturbing happened.

I should say at this point that I in no way hold my parents responsible for what occurred. I know their intentions were good. They just got it horribly wrong.

On January 26, 1980, Thomas junior's seventh birthday arrived, bringing what should have been a seminal moment in his Norwich City-supporting journey – his very first Canaries' kit. And I did get a shirt. It was made by the manufacturer who made the Norwich kit: Admiral. It had the trademark Admiral logo running down the sleeves, with the striped trim on the V-neck and the collar. But that's unfortunately where the similarities ended. It was a Leeds United shirt

In my parents' defence, they knew how much I wanted to be able to turn up to football practice in a proper football kit and a kind and well-meaning family from my old man's church harked from West Yorkshire and were big Leeds fans. Somewhere along the line my football kit plight had been mentioned and they very kindly passed on a full kit that one of their boys had out-grown.

Had I faced this situation a few years later I would have vented my disgust at my parents for even thinking this was appropriate. But at the age of seven I was happy that at long last I had something proper to wear, although whenever I was asked why I was in a Leeds kit, I struggled for an answer. Admitting to it being a hand-me-down from a family who had taken pity on me wasn't an option, and it was 11 long months before I could finally stop inadvertently supporting that team from West Yorkshire!

On Christmas Day 1980 it was *deja-vu* as I picked up the soft, similar sized present from under the tree but this time, when I ripped open the wrapping, I was hit by the flash of vibrant green and yellow within. I loved the Admiral trim it had down the arms, the green cuffs with the yellow stripes, the V-necked collar and the understated Admiral logo. And so, like so many kids (and big kids) down the years, I remained in my kit for the rest of that Christmas day and many days beyond. There's something special about your first ever football kit. In my case, there was something special about my second football kit!

A CARROW ROAD DEBUT

My years at *Blue Peter* gave me a huge opportunity to engage with the club in ways I would never have dreamed. My link with Norfolk and especially Carrow Road was something they were keen to explore and represent on the show – much to my delight.

On a kids' show like *Blue Peter*, you know you have a fairly short shelf-life. The days of 12-year tenures (*a la* John Noakes) were long gone, with most presenters averaging around four to five years. I made it clear that once my time on *Blue Peter* was up, sports broadcasting was what I wanted to pursue. My colleagues were more than happy to support me in this and I remain hugely thankful.

In 2001, I made a *Blue Peter* film as a guest summariser on BBC Radio Norfolk's match-day coverage of Norwich against Crewe. The idea was to put me in the commentary box alongside Roy Waller and find out if I could cut the mustard as a match summariser, the sort of role now being filled by the likes of Darren Eadie and Adam Drury – the difference being that while I was a recognisable voice and name, I was anything but a practised football pundit.

I've never been afraid of making a fool of myself (it's a prerequisite for *Blue Peter*) and it was going to be fun, interesting and probably amusing for viewers to see Thomas floundering in a commentary box, but I wasn't so sure the Radio Norfolk's match-day audience would see the funny side.

Before the actual game, *Blue Peter* wanted to film me getting some tips from one of the BBC's main radio commentators. So they decided to go for Alan Green – at Portman Road! I tried to say that this was a really bad idea on a whole number of levels, not least because this was one of those rare periods when Ipswich were enjoying playing in a league higher than Norwich. My indignation fell on deaf ears.

In the end, my foray behind enemy lines proved uneventful. In pre-Twitter days it was much easier to keep a low profile. I covered up in a big coat and hat, so the first most Ipswich fans would know about my trip to Portman Road was when the film went out a few weeks later, which was probably a good thing as I had to sit there watching the Tractor Boys beat Leicester 2-0. They would end the season in fifth and in Europe. How times change!

Four weeks later I was back in the more familiar and pleasant surroundings of Carrow Road ready for my summarising debut alongside Mr Waller.

Now, in the last five seasons fronting Sky Sports' Football League coverage, I have presented well over 300 games and I have got my preparation notes down to a fine art. In 2001, I had never put together notes for a football match in my life, but as a lifelong adherer to the *'fail to prepare, prepare to fail'* maxim, I did as much homework as I could, especially about the opposition, Crewe Alexandra, who I hadn't seen an awful lot of. However, I didn't see this as a major problem as I was there to summarise rather than commentate. I'd leave Roy to call the game, and I would simply attempt to offer my limited wisdom on the finer points of this big second tier clash as 12th-placed Norwich took on 20th-placed Crewe.

I arrived at Carrow Road with the *Blue Peter* crew in plenty of time. We filmed the customary piece to camera outside the ground to set up the day and headed in to meet Roy.

I have a great admiration for commentators. I always tell anyone who asks about my job fronting Sky's Football League coverage that the most skilful and hardest working people on a live game are the commentators. They have to be able to recognise all of the players in a split second – a momentary check of the notes is often not an option as the game moves so quickly. They not only have to talk for 90 minutes or more, but they have to describe the action in a way that both informs and enlightens the viewer or listener. They also have to make a call, like a referee, in a split second on the big moments of the game and all this while trying to avoid all the usual football clichés. It really is some skill.

I remember sitting there with Roy while we filmed a chat between the two of us about the day ahead, the game, the two teams, the form of both, the key players and so on. Then we gathered with the rest of the assembled local media to make a note of the two teams that Nigel Worthington and Dario Gradi had gone with. Fortunately for me with my amateurish preparation notes there were no changes for a Crewe side who featured Mark Rivers in midfield, and a 17-year-old called Dean Ashton on the bench. For Norwich there was just the one change; Paul McVeigh coming in for the injured Iwan Roberts.

I remember a rather sick feeling in my stomach as we both

made the short journey from the press room to the famous commentary position above the tunnel in the City Stand, where I sat there and took it all in. I thought about the days when a trip to Carrow Road was a rare treat, and the notion of being in the commentary box would have been laughable.

It was only a brief moment of reminiscing and self-congratulation though. The teams gathered in the tunnel, Roy got his cue from the presenter Matthew Gudgin in the Radio Norfolk studio and we were on.

After his usual introduction to the game and the teams, Roy introduced his guest summariser for the week. I took my cue and blathered on about how good it was to be there, how good it was to be sat next to a seasoned pro like Roy and how much I was looking forward to a mouth-watering clash.

The goal-less first half was largely bland on the pitch and also, thankfully, unexciting from my point of view. There were no big incidents, no moments of real controversy for me to make some kind of sense of.

But on about 50 minutes Roy said, 'Well I've done a lot of commentating, I think that's over to you now'. What?? That really was not in the script. But when you're live on the radio, you get on with it, and as I uttered my opening, unremarkable words, I asked Roy to be ready to mark me out of ten.

I wish I hadn't.

Unlike television commentary, where you can allow the pictures to do the talking, radio doesn't afford you that time or space. If you stop talking, the listener doesn't have a clue what's going on. While the ball was with Norwich, all was OK. When the ball fell to Crewe, by the time I'd looked down at my team sheet to make sure I didn't get the name of the number nine wrong, the ball had moved on via two more players. It was a nightmare. And then Crewe scored and I got the scorer wrong.

I wanted to gather my notes, gently put down my headphones, bid a silent farewell to Roy and head off into the gloom, but – being the gracious and consummate pro – Roy picked up the commentary as if nothing had happened. He was incredibly gracious. I doubt the listeners at home were feeling as generous but I like to think Chris Llewellyn's late equaliser eased their frustrations a little!

In many ways, that afternoon at Carrow Road in the February gloom was an invaluable early insight into the world of sports broadcasting in which I now happily, and more confidently, find myself. Roy made it look easy that day. It was seamless. But that came from not just years of doing the job, but the work he put in to every match. He was a gentleman that day and that was a trait that marked his life and his 30 years on the Norfolk airwaves. He loved his football but most importantly he loved his club. I was covering the World Cup in South Africa when I learnt of his passing and as I read the reams of tributes, one summed the sad moment up perfectly: 'a little piece of Norfolk has been lost'.

On the times I have returned to Carrow Road in my role with Sky I often find myself looking at the now empty commentating position over the tunnel, and cast my mind back to that day in February all those years ago, and the gentleman who was at my side.

A TEST OF NERVES

I can't explain why, but from an early stage in the 2014-15 season I had an unshakeable hunch that destiny would bring Norwich and Ipswich together in the play-offs. Very early on, I asked my Football League producer, Stevie Rowe, whether, hypothetically, I would still have to present the play-off final if the two East Anglian rivals were to meet at Wembley. The answer was, 'Of course'.

Fast forward several months and I was at the iPro Stadium on the final day of the regular season to witness Derby County blowing up inexplicably against a poor Reading side. Results elsewhere meant Norwich would play you-know-who in the play-off semi-finals and, as I got in the car to drive home, I reeled slightly at the prospect of the biggest test of my football-presenting career. Come what may, I would soon be at Wembley for the final with either my team or, heaven forbid, Ipswich Town! And, before that, I would have to present the two biggest East Anglian derbies ever.

One week later I woke up in a hotel a stone's throw from Portman Road. The pre-game Twitter banter with Ipswich fans had been fairly quiet and good humoured – the best of the week being a fan who had photo-shopped one of my Sky publicity photos, replacing my suit with an Ipswich shirt! But I sensed they were nervous and regarded the first home leg as an absolute must-win.

Those thoughts were shared by former Town boss George Burley and Darren Eadie who joined me in the studio for the game. As the ground filled and the players warmed up and our on-air time of noon moved ever closer, I suddenly felt overwhelmed by an unexpected attack of nerves. Normally I don't get fazed about the prospect of live television. But at almost the last possible moment my heart rate went into orbit, my palms turned sweaty and it dawned on me in a new way not just the magnitude of the game, but the fact I was about to present the bloody thing! Everyone watching would be looking out for even the tiniest hint of bias. As the countdown in my ear began, it was genuinely one of the most nervous moments I've had in sports broadcasting – even worse than that horrible moment Roy had asked me to commentate!

People often ask how I remain impartial covering big games that have involved my team. It's not easy but the idea is that when the moment arrives to 'go live', a subconscious switch flicks in my head, all emotional attachments are suspended and I focus on the mechanics of presenting the show.

For example, at start of the season when Ipswich and Norwich resumed battle after a three-year separation, I was in the studio with James Scowcroft and Eadie. When Lewis Grabban scored for Norwich after 24 minutes, Eadie jumped to his feet in celebration, Scowcroft looked to the floor and I didn't flinch. Inside, deep down somewhere, I was screaming for joy, yet not a flicker of this reached the surface. I just turned to my notes and wrote down the time of the goal and that it was Grabban's fourth goal in his first four games for the club. On that occasion, the switch worked like a dream. The Play-Offs, on the other hand, proved a sterner test!

As Ipswich and Norwich kicked off on Saturday lunchtime in that marvellous May of 2015, I, like all the fans, was on the edge of my seat. I'd somehow, despite the nerves, managed to find the words to steer the programme to kick-off, but the proper business was now finally underway. I very quickly realised it was going to be impossible to watch this game in the same way I did in the calmer waters of the August meeting. And, sure enough, when Jonny Howson scored, my professionalism deserted me. I leapt out of my seat and let out a primeval kind of 'YESSSSSSSS!' that left our sound engineer in the TV truck outside with a pair of sore ears and George Burley with a less than amused look.

When Paul Anderson equalised it was time for Burley to leap from his studio chair while Messieurs Eadie and Thomas looked on at the masses of Ipswich fans now goading us through the studio window. Darren gave as good as he got while I simply looked down dutifully, noted the scorer and began to think about what I'd be saying going into the break at half time.

Let's be honest, the second half wasn't one that will live long in the memory but as the curtain came down on the first leg I think most Ipswich fans feared (and Norwich fans sincerely hoped) that their best chance was gone. In the cauldron of noise that would await at Carrow Road a week later it was going to take something special from Mick McCarthy's side to secure an end of season party at Wembley.

The following Friday I was at the Riverside to watch a very impressive Middlesbrough book their place in the play-off final by beating Brentford and my head did not hit the pillow of my room in the Holiday Inn at Carrow Road until around 3.15am.

I was counting on a restorative five or six hours sleep but a rogue alarm call from the hotel went off at 6am. That was it. Immediately my mind was buzzing with a million thoughts of what lay ahead and there was no chance of getting back to sleep. As I opened my curtains and looked over the Carrow Road pitch with a moody early morning gloom overhead, my mind wandered back to my first trip to Carrow Road and tried to imagine what that seven-year-old boy would have thought if he'd been told that 35 years later he'd be at the same ground presenting this hugest of derbies between Norwich and Ipswich.

Thankfully, there was no repeat attack of nerves as we went on air for the second leg and I think part of that was down to good old home comforts. But I also had this really strong feeling that Norwich were going to pull this off. In the days leading up to the second leg, all I'd seen from the impressive Alex Neil and his players was a calm confidence. It wasn't arrogance or complacency; they just looked like a group of players who knew that if they kept their heads, were patient and did what they did best, their trip to the Wembley final was assured.

The scenes in the studio high up in the Jarrold Stand that

day followed the pattern of the week before. For the second week running, I just couldn't hold it in. Darren and I leapt out of our seats in unison numerous times as that electric second half sent Carrow Road delirious and Norwich booked their place in the final. It was an unforgettable day and every time I've looked back at the highlights of that Saturday I just feel that happy glow of pride in our wonderful club.

But later, as I walked back to the hotel with the lack of sleep taking effect and adrenaline waning, my mind turned to what the next weekend now held. Presenting three play-off finals over three days, culminating in the Championship final... featuring my team!

It would be fair to say that by the time that magic Monday arrived I'd had plenty of time to soak up the play-off final atmosphere, having done the League Two final on the Saturday and League One game on the Sunday. It was still stirring, however, as I walked down Wembley Way after Preston had thrashed Swindon in the Sunday match and saw the stallholders beginning to bring out the colours of the two teams who would bring the 2014-15 Football League season to a climax. The moment had almost arrived. Resisting the temptation to join some of my Sky colleagues at the hotel bar, I headed to my room to run through my script once again and make sure that the words I had written for our build-up to the game would do justice to what is always a big day, but was absolutely massive for my club and for me.

Like all who were there, there are so many memories of that day that I could fill another book with them, so here are just a few highlights.

We had decided to present the start and finish of the show pitch-side at Wembley and so with about 20 minutes to go, and Norwich still 2-0 up we made our way from the studio back down to the tunnel. That meant I had a 'ringside' view of the climax and one of the great moments in the history of Norwich City Football Club.

I stood to the right of the tunnel entrance and took in the view. To my left, the Norwich squad and backroom staff were sitting, feverishly checking the clock. Roger East, the fourth official stood just in front of me. He too was constantly checking his stopwatch. Beyond him, Gary Holt and Alex Neil paced the touchline.

With seconds to go, Ricky Martin, the club's technical director, leaned over, shook my hand and shouted, 'See you tonight! See you tonight!' And that was when referee Mike Dean brought his whistle to his lips. Norwich had done it. They had won at Wembley. They were back in the Premier League.

I knew I had to flick that switch, get back into work mode and re-focus on the 45 minutes or so on air we had to come. But I took a moment to take in what I was witnessing. To be so close to my team as the celebrations began, and to the chorus of the thousands of euphoric Norwich fans, was an unforgettable experience. I shall savour it for the rest of my life.

When the work ended I felt torn because the Championship play-off final marks the end of a long season for Sky's Football League team and means a well-earned night out. But I couldn't stop thinking about Ricky Martin's invitation to the best party in town. I headed into central London with my work colleagues. It was the right thing to do because at that moment it was about showing my gratitude to a lot of the people behind the scenes who make Sky's coverage of the Football League work for ten months of the year.

But my heart was still at Wembley and after a few end-of-season refreshments somewhere in Soho, as I sat with colleagues reliving the day's events, one of them said, 'I can see in your face where you'd rather be, you should go. Days like this don't happen very often'. I looked around the table for some kind of reassurance and everyone said, 'You've got to go'. Minutes later Bill Leslie, who had commentated on the match, and I were in a cab heading back to Wembley. And so the day ended with a rather late entry to the Norwich promotion party at the Hilton Hotel by the stadium.

I have many wonderful (albeit slightly hazy) memories of that night. I might owe Alex Neil and the players an apology for saying too many times how amazing I thought they were. The next morning I awoke, back home with the Norwich scarf Elliott Bennett had put round my neck lying by the bed, a smile on my face, a slightly fuzzy head and wondering whether all of what had gone before had really happened.

I will never experience a day quite like it again. There will be more highs and inevitable lows to come, but to see my team perform like that on the big stage, to secure promotion in the most emphatic of ways and to witness it through the privileged role my job involves made it a day I will treasure for ever.

One more thing. I began my 'Tale' by recounting how I saw my sister just before kick-off. Well, I have a photo I took that day of the Norwich City fans behind our presenting position. It was from those moments just before we went on air and there amongst the happy faces is my sister Becky and her family smiling down and waving excitedly. I was at work, but I did get to share the day with my family and the Norwich City family and, as for many of you, that was the best bit of all.

Simon Thomas, a former *Blue Peter* presenter, grew up in a Norfolk village and defied peer pressure to support his local team. He is Sky Sports' lead presenter for live coverage of Football League matches.

8

Norwich supporters had a special song for **Paul McVeigh**, but it was not love at first sight. In fact, after surviving a three-day trial at the beginning of his City career, it was more than a season later before he finally established himself in the first team and in the affections of the fans.

This is a story of persistence, of refusing to be floored by life's knocks – and of one appearance as a substitute that altered everything.

TWENTY MINUTES THAT
CHANGED MY CAREER

BY PAUL McVEIGH

The idea that I might try to become a Norwich City player began with a brief conversation with a Welshman by the name of Gwyn Walters, the education officer at Spurs. I'd just been told they didn't want me and I was desperate to find another club quickly. Gwyn mentioned that I might work well with another Welsh guy named Iwan Roberts at Norwich City – and I said, 'Iwan who?'

The big man, who I now call a good friend and with whom I had the most successful partnership of my career, will probably slap me for that throwaway comment but unfortunately in my bubble of arrogance/innocence at Tottenham Hotspur I was unaware of the cult status that Robbo was building at Norwich City.

In fact, at that moment, I wasn't aware of much at all other than my devastation about the fact that Spurs didn't want me. I'd received that news when manager George Graham sat me down in his office and told me that I wasn't what he was looking for. In other words, 'Get out of my office, shorty, and stop bothering me'. I do understand that George Graham liked his players to be six feet plus but he had me in his squad a few times and played me in the reserves, where I was top scorer for two seasons. And I was same the height when Spurs hired me as when they fired me. It wasn't as if I'd suddenly shrunk.

To say I was floored is an understatement. I had just been released from a club that I loved playing for. When I finally picked myself up off the floor both mentally and emotionally I knew that I needed to get myself to another club and sharpish. So after Gwyn suggested playing alongside Iwan somebody at Norwich, I telephoned Bryan Hamilton, who had just taken over as manager at Carrow Road.

'Hammy' was from Belfast, like me. He'd had a spell as Northern Ireland manager and I'd played for the national under-21 team, so I had a slim relationship with him already. Our telephone conversation led to me being offered a three-day trial. Driving up the A11 from London to 'the Fine City', I naively thought that, as I was going to a team that I had barely heard of, I would inevitably earn myself a contract. Boy, was I in for a shock.

Neal Fenn, who I knew from his time at Spurs, had been at Norwich on loan and had told me about the set-up, but I still wasn't ready for the shock of arriving at the Colney training complex and discovering the facilities were as good as Spurs Lodge. And there wasn't a tractor to be seen! Unfortunately for me, that wasn't the biggest wake up call I received that day in March 2000.

Walking into the changing room on the first day of my trial was incredibly daunting. Of course, I did not know that these people would go on to become some of my best friends in football; I just saw players of the calibre of Malky Mackay and Mike Milligan, who were in 'compost corner'. That was the area of the dressing room where players who were not getting much match action congregated. In other words, they felt they'd been left to rot.

Looking around the rest of the room, there also were seriously good players, like Craig Bellamy, Craig Fleming and a good friend from Belfast Phil Mulryne. Incidentally, at that stage, you could have got extremely long odds on Phil eventually becoming a priest! And once we started training, I began to realise that folk might not necessarily bet on me to become a Norwich player. I realised, too, that I should have heard about the guy called Iwan Roberts.

I was surprised how much enjoyment the players were having and how relaxed it seemed, but the biggest shock was the quality on show. When Bellars and Robbo did some extra shooting practice at the end of training, and smashed home virtually every chance past Andy Marshall and a young Rob Green, I just had to stand back and admire what I saw.

I remember having a conversation with the first team coach, Steve Foley, afterwards about the relaxed attitude of training. He said that Kenny Dalglish had a saying: 'Have a laugh in training but don't make training a laugh'. I thought that expression summed up those three days of my trial perfectly. 'Enjoy what you are doing but remember that you still need to work your socks off to succeed'.

The ironic thing about Dalglish's senior's catchphrase was that his son Paul took the 'have a laugh in training' part to extremes when he was at Norwich. For example, one day, when the newly installed nutritionist was having one-to-ones with all the players, Paul turned up to his meeting with a McDonald's in one hand and a milkshake in the other and asked, 'So where do you think I am going wrong?' Her retort was that he needed to introduce more fruit and vegetables into his diet: all very sound advice indeed for any normal professional footballer. But Daggers asked, straight-faced, 'Will eating a banana improve my touch?' and left the poor nutritionist exasperated!

Anyway, one extremely good thing that stood out for me on that memorable first day of my Norwich trial was the warmth of the staff at the training ground: people like Val Lemmon who was the PA, confidante and all-round saviour of the manager. Val would virtually become my surrogate mum, as I was in her office every day after training telling her all my problems and 99 times out of 100 she solved them for me. Then there was the physio Tim 'Hasselhoff' Sheppard (kindly nick-named by Paul Dalglish because of his alleged resemblance to the Baywatch star). His assistant physio, Keithy Creamer, was one of the nicest guys you could wish to meet, and the wizened kit man Terry Postle was a star. All these people seemed to be batting for me to win the contract, and that added to my determination.

That first day at Colney I knew that it was the only place for me. Call it instinct or a gut feeling but I knew it would be the place where I could thrive. And so, after three days that flew by, I had a very different experience in a manager's office to the one that had signalled the end of my Spurs days. Believe me when I tell you all managers' offices look the same – sort of tired and well-used. It was me who looked different when I came out, because I had a huge grin and an offer of a one-year contract at Norwich City.

The prospect of being a first team player seemed much more tangible to me at Norwich City because I saw so many players that I felt on a par with breaking into and playing reg-ularly in the starting eleven: guys like Darren Kenton, Darel Russell and Chris Llewellyn. And, even though Phil Mulryne had signed from Manchester United and Paul Dalglish from Newcastle United, I felt very quickly that these were my peers.

If that sounds cocky, what I mean was that part of my problem at Spurs had been that I always saw the likes of Teddy Sheringham, Jurgen Klinsmann, 'Sir' Les Ferdinand and David 'the best looking man I have ever met in football' Ginola as my superiors. I respected and admired the quality of the Norwich players, but now I could allow myself to believe more in my own ability too.

I made my first team debut a couple of months later, away to Bolton, but life wasn't instantly a bed of roses at Norwich

City, despite the fact that though I very quickly felt part of the furniture (especially in Val's office where I was always getting under her feet). It took quite a while for me to establish myself in the first team and there was to be a real low before it happened.

Bryan Hamilton only lasted seven months, and three of those were the close-season! Another fellow Irishman came in to take the hot seat: Nigel Worthington. I didn't know Nigel beforehand but thought his appointment was a good sign. After all, there can't be too many clubs who have successive Northern Irish managers, so I thought, 'I must be at the right place'. But it actually took much longer than a while to establish myself in the team. I learned that I had done enough to earn another one-year contract but not enough to win a regular place in the starting 11.

I must admit I had some tearful conversations down the phone to my parents. I told them that I just didn't think that a career in football was worth pursuing. I was training all week long but then had to watch the 'proper' players go off to play in stadia all over the country while I got weekends off. I was going nowhere, literally. Sometimes I played for the 'stiffs' (reserve team) during the week in front of one man and often even his dog couldn't be bothered to come and watch!

A season in the reserves was the last thing I wanted but that's exactly what I got under Worthington. It felt that I couldn't do enough to impress the manager or, more accurately, whatever I was doing wasn't enough to make my breakthrough. I was first into Colney in the morning and generally one of three last players to leave. Invariably, it would be Bellamy, Green and me staying in the gym trying our bests to get stronger and improve. One afternoon when the three of us were finishing a session, I gathered enough confidence to tell Bellars, jokingly, that it was only a matter of time before I took his place. In his usual cocky manner, Bellars said 'you can have it because I'll be playing in the Premier League'! That was the kind of self-confidence that I simply didn't have but admired so much in Craig. He didn't just hope to make it in the Premier League. He one hundred per cent knew that it was his divine right to play for some of the best clubs in the top division.

But Norwich were in the second tier and, if the truth be told, I don't think I was at the physical level that was required to play in one of the most demanding divisions in the world. Not that I had the self-awareness in my first 12 months at Norwich City. I thought scoring some goals in the reserves should have been enough to get me into the first team. Alas, I was way off.

One Monday January morning I was summoned to the manager's office for a meeting. I strolled into the room, honestly believing that I was going to be getting my big chance that weekend against Watford at home. What transpired was possibly the last scenario that entered my head.

I sat down in front of Worthy, ready for the good news, but the words that left the manager's lips will never, ever be erased from my memory.

'I'm letting you go wee man.'

'You're what?'

'I think you need to find another club.'

'But why? I'm working as hard as anyone at this club.'

'Because I don't think you have what it takes.'

I was absolutely gutted. Telling me he was letting me go was bad enough. Saying I didn't have the ability or attitude or … 'it', well, that was like someone forcing a knife into my stomach and twisting it round.

I didn't agree with what Nigel Worthington's assessment of me was back then and I obviously don't agree with him today, when I can look back at some real achievements with Norwich. But as much as it pains me to admit it he did have a point. In hindsight, feeling on a par with the senior players at Norwich City (as opposed to believing myself inferior, as I had at Tottenham) worked both for and against me. It gave me confidence in my ability, which a footballer must have, but my work ethic simply wasn't what was required to get to the top level of professional football.

But my journey to being in the team for the 2002 play-off final at Cardiff started that day I walked out of Nigel Worthington's office, 17 months earlier, having been told my fledgling career at the club was over. I was distraught as I left the manager's office but being as stubborn as I was (and am), I knew that I couldn't give up on my dream of having a long-term future in the professional game.

Craig Fleming was the first player that I told what had happened and he was extremely supportive. Straight away he gave the Oldham manager, Andy Ritchie, a call and organised for me to go on trial the following Monday. He also arranged for me to have a few days at Bury for them to have a look at me.

But the footballing gods must have been looking down on me that week. Suddenly, a few Norwich regulars could not get over injuries and I received a call on the Thursday from the manager to say I would need to be sub that Saturday against Watford at Carrow Road. True to his word, I was indeed a named substitute but I believed I was there just to make up the numbers with the players who he actually did want. Yet with 20 minutes remaining in the game, and with Norwich 0-1 down, Worthy decided to do the unthinkable and put me on for what should have been my last ever appearance at Carrow Road. It was to be 20 minutes that changed my life.

I gave everything that I could. I was dribbling down the left wing and taking players on, I was tracking back... even making tackles (and as many of you will remember, tackling wasn't something I repeated very often before or after that day). In the 81st minute, I picked up the ball on the left and dribbled past one, two, three players and drove a left footed diagonal ball for Steen Nedergaard to score a looping header!

Now Steen was the nicest guy in football. How nice? Well, Norwich played Man City in their last season at Maine Road and Steen was playing right wing against Stuart Pearce, who was in the twilight of his career and operating in his familiar left back berth. Steen picked up the ball and nimbly glided past the red-faced Pearce who duly took Steeno out somewhere near the patella. As Steen lies on the floor, gasping for air, Pearcy leans down over the top of Steen and screams in his face 'get up you dirty cheat'! Facing up from the floor, the Dane and long-term Forest fan replied 'Stuart, you used to be my favourite player'. With his finger in Steen's face, Psycho moved in closer and roars 'I still bloody well am' and jogged on!

Anyway, after Mr Nice Guy had headed home my cross that day against Watford, Lee Marshall scored the winner with two minutes to go. I must say, there is no better feeling in football than when you think you are going to lose a game but, in the dying minutes, your team steals the victory out of the jaws of defeat. Carrow Road erupted and as the final whistle went the entire team was applauded off. And, as I walked towards the tunnel, I wondered to myself whether that really was going to be last appearance at that stadium in front of those amazing fans.

I trooped into the dressing room where the celebrations were already in full swing. But I didn't feel like joining in. I was already thinking about what life could be like if I were to sign at Bury or Oldham. I quietly got changed and went to leave the changing room. I had to pass the spot where Worthy was getting changed. Just as I tried to walk past him, he put his arm out and physically stopped me from leaving.

'You're not going anywhere Macca, you did well out there

today. You just need to come in on Monday get your head down and work hard'.

At that precise moment my career path altered forever. I knew that what he had said to me in his office wasn't true and I had shown a glimpse of what I could do out on the biggest stage. But I knew too that he was right about one thing: I did need to get my head down. In that moment, I understood that my commitment to my career and Norwich city needed to go up ten fold. And it did.

I decided that going out with my mates and enjoying myself needed to be a distant second in my priorities to having a proper, professional football career. Technically, of course, I was already having a professional football career but it was not the sort of career that I had in mind. I wanted to be starting regularly, be the top scorer, the main man. If I wanted those kind of results in my life then I knew I needed to take massive action.

I only knew this esoteric knowledge because I read a book when I was 17 entitled '*Awaken The Giant Within*', (I hope you can see the irony) by an American guy, Anthony Robbins. Even from that early age I had my career and life mapped out in my head, which included how many games I wanted to play in my career (500 in case you're wondering), how much money I wanted to earn per week (£10,000 in case you're nosey) and other long term goals such as running my own business and writing a book (*The Stupid Footballer is Dead* in case you haven't got around to buying it).

I had read the Robbins book while I was at Spurs but for whatever reason – maturity, experience or desperation – it was that day in January 2001 that I decided I needed to change everything I was doing. Starting with my mindset.

The question that I use now in my company, ThinkPRO, when I am working with young professional footballers who are looking to carve out careers for themselves in football is the same question that I asked myself, repeatedly, in January 2001 as I set out to make a massive change in my life and career. Whatever I was doing I asked myself 'Is this going to help me achieve my dreams?'

That single question helped me give up alcohol for two years from the age of 21 to 23. It helped me change my eating habits. It was the catalyst for the way I trained in the off season (knowing I needed to go back not just as fit but fitter than the previous season). All these powerful outcomes came from one question, simple but hugely effective.

Clearly, these kind of changes don't happen overnight but the accumulative effect allowed me to return for the start of the 2001-02 season not as a boy any more but as a man ready to compete physically, technically and, most importantly, psychologically with the other first team players in Norwich and beyond.

The first game of that eventful season was away at Millwall. It was a 4-0 mauling! Anyone who was there that day probably still has nightmares because from the first to the last minute it was awful. Our next game was at home against Manchester City, who were strongly fancied to get promoted that year under the stewardship of Kevin Keegan (and who had a young lad from Lincoln as an unused sub on that day: 'D Huckerby').

In football, as in life, when one door closes another door opens. In this case, it was the misfortune of our left-winger Chris Llewellyn, our most saleable asset that season, to have the door closed – in his face. Ten minutes into the game, Chris collided with a Man City defender, injured his cheekbone, was taken off and was rushed to hospital and diagnosed with a fractured cheekbone. You wouldn't wish that on your worst enemy never mind one of your friends and teammates but, looking back all these years later, that was a pivotal moment in both of our seasons, and in my Norwich City career.

Worthy threw me on down the left wing (where he had used me during pre-season in Scotland just a few weeks earlier) and not only did we go on to beat the eventual division winners 2-0 but we produced a top class performance that was embodied by one man: Marc Libbra. He came on as a sub and, just 19 seconds later, flicked the ball over Steve Howie's head and drilled it into the bottom right hand corner past Nicky Weaver. The whole of Carrow Road exploded with euphoria, and so did my head. Then I managed to score the second goal to seal the victory and, at last, had exactly the feeling I'd imagined as a young boy in the back streets of Belfast when I longed to be a professional footballer.

There can't be many better ways to impress the fans of your new team than what Libbra did that day, but he never again matched that excellence. For me, though, that game and my goal were the start of a period when everything seemed to go right: my purple patch in yellow. Scoring the only goal of the game at Bradford and looping a header into the far top corner against Wolves in the play-off semi were among numerous highlights from a special season.

I was delighted for the club and the players that the Norwich City class of 2015 experienced the play-offs. Getting to the final feels like a real reward for a fantastic team effort all season long. Of course, Alex Neil's men had a considerably better feeling coming away from Wembley in May 2015 than we did walking out of the Millennium Stadium in Cardiff when we lost to Birmingham on penalties in 2002.

But going through the complete spectrum of emotions in our final in 2002 really brought the squad closer together. Everything from Robbo's delicate header into the corner of the net and that iconic picture of the big man sliding away on his knees in sheer delight through to the despair of the boys who missed their penalties. Each moment contributed to building a bond within that group of players that was incredibly special.

Playing for Norwich meant that every one of the team lived close enough to the city so that we could all socialise together. This is so rare in football as players from most other clubs generally don't see each other outside of training and games because of the large distances most players commute on a daily basis. Being able to work and play with my mates was a common theme throughout my entire time at Norwich City.

And, going out in the city with a large group of teammates, I would inevitably hear cries of 'Iwan!, Iwan!, Iwan!' In all the years that I've now spent in Norfolk, the only other player who could give Robbo a run for his money as a fans' favourite was Grant Holt – and I certainly didn't guess the impact Holty would have the first time I came across him.

I left Norwich in 2007 and had two years at Luton. In 2009, Bryan Gunn re-signed me and, when I went for my medical, I found myself sitting next to the club's new centre-forward from Shrewsbury. I must admit I didn't think this guy was going to go on and be top scorer three years in succession and have a hat-trick of player of the year awards. In fact, I thought he looked more like the new groundsman!

Coming back to sign a one year contract in 2009 under Bryan Gunn felt like I was coming home. It had been horrible to watch my team fall into League One but sometimes in life you need to take a step backwards to take two forwards. That was exactly what happened under the new guidance of new manager Paul Lambert. And then some!

When Lambo came into the meeting room on his first day and told us in his broken English that we were going to win the League (I needed to translate for some of the lads) I thought he was off his rocker! Sitting third from bottom wasn't the normal starting point for a charge at the title. But that is exactly what happened. All I can say is that the unbeaten run, as well as the free flowing attacking football that we played that season was amazing. I'm using a lot of artistic licence when I say 'we' though. I was on the bench so much that season I used to take a cushion and blanket! But at least I had a good view as Wes Hoolahan, Chris Martin, Holty and the rest destroyed teams with quality, power and guile.

Our feeder club, Leeds United, gave us a good run for our money that season but I don't think there was ever any real doubt. We had Russell Martin at the back playing out of his skin as usual, Fraser Forster pulling off saves from every conceivable angle and some terrific squad players like Matty Gill, Anthony McNamee and Korey Smith.

Being part of that 2009-10 League One winning squad was a fantastic experience, especially as I decided to retire at the end of it. But although I have a division winners medal from that season I didn't feel like I fully earned it. Paul Lambert involved me in every squad, but unless you are out on the pitch doing your bit it is difficult to feel like you are contributing. Compare it to my other Football League winners medal and it is like night and day!

Coming off the back of a play-off final in 2001-02 and being top goal scorer in 2002-03, I felt on top of my game going into the 2003-04 campaign. But the first half of the season was a bit up and down until the loan signings of Peter Crouch, Kevin Harper and a certain Darren Huckerby showed that we could really challenge.

The home game against Cardiff on December 13, 2003 was the day that held our season in the balance: Hucks's last game on loan. Would he go or stay? He decided that, if he was leaving, he'd go out with a bang. Picking the ball up on the half way line normally doesn't mean a goal scoring opportunity but when you have pace to burn and a gap in the opposition defence then maybe it is! Hucks knocked the ball through the two centre halves, gave the defenders about a ten-yard head start and still beat them to the ball before slotting it away. Sensational. As Phil Mulryne and I tried to catch Hucks to celebrate, all I could say to my good mate Phil was 'why don't they just hurry up and sign him?!'

These things are never straightforward of course, and a lot of work needed to be done to make the transfer from Manchester City happen. The talking went on up until Christmas Day and, while it was happening, the club signed Leon McKenzie, who introduced himself with two goals at Ipswich. So we went 'top of the League at Portman Road', as the song goes. And then, on Boxing Day, before the Carrow Road match against Forest, it was announced that Hucks was going to be a Norwich player.

For the record, if he had not signed, then I don't think we would have been promoted. We were a strong, solid team all over the pitch. But Hucks gave us that extra bit of quality that helped us retain top spot for the rest of the season.

Being in the squad that took Norwich City back into the Premier League was a personal highlight and, for the club, the culmination of the work of a number of years. There were so many highs and lows in that Premier League season of 2004-05 but one particular moment stood out for me more than any other – when I scored against Man Utd at Old Trafford. If you haven't seen it, it was a simple goal really.

There was a long-ball up field from Rob Green to our centre-half come striker Gary Doherty. The Ginger Pele laid the ball off to me on the right wing. I brushed off a player called Cristiano Ronaldo, which was no mean feat because he was extremely greasy in those days. Then Roy Keane came towards me, so I nutmegged him and kept dribbling towards the United goal at the Stretford End. Out of nowhere, Bobby

Charlton slid in, but I flicked it over his legs, avoiding his comb-over as it whipped past my eyes. I looked across to the bench and saw Georgie Best, who was chatting up some girl in the crowd. Then there was only Peter Schmeichel to beat. He came rushing out at me and just like Phillipe Albert did for New-castle, I dinked it over the top of the red nosed git and then celebrated like I'd just won the World Cup… even though we were still 2-1 down! I may have slightly embellished that story. It does seem to get better every year.

Okay, here's the reality. The ball was knocked down, I scuffed at it with my left foot and somehow it went into the top corner, past Tim Howard.

And really, there is no need for me to embellish my Norwich story. I will always be immensely proud to have played along-side some truly great players in some special teams and to have been a part, however small, of a wonderful club.

Paul McVeigh had two spells at Norwich, and in each of them won a medal for winning a division of the Football League. After finishing playing he was a co-presenter on Radio Norfolk before moving into national broadcasting, writing a book about the psychology of success and delivering motivational training and speeches.

9

Chris Goreham knows his job on Radio Norfolk is the envy of many, and he is pretty pleased with it himself – especially as he supports the team whose fortunes he describes.

But, as he explains, some of the logistics are challenging and some of the facilities have been rudimentary.

And then there was the task of tackling a manager who was a ticking time-bomb. The biggest test, though, came when the Norwich manager was a friend and former colleague.

GAFFER TAPE AND STICKY SITUATIONS

BY CHRIS GOREHAM

'It is raining very hard now and the players are coming off the field.' If I told you that was a line from my first BBC commentary you might assume I started my career on *Test Match Special*. But there wasn't a cake in sight at Carrow Road on Saturday, July 29, 2000 as Norwich City played the Dutch club SC Heerenveen in a low-wattage pre-season friendly.

Not that it felt unimportant to me.

The bosses at BBC Radio Norfolk had been good enough to give me a chance to share commentary duties with the great Roy Waller, the voice of the station's football coverage for almost 20 years by that point. I was 18 years old but that's what pre-season friendlies are all about: having a look at a young upstart in a game that doesn't really matter before ruffling his hair and sending him back to play with his friends when the real stuff starts. I can see that now but as Roy passed his headphones to me and announced to whatever audience that game had managed to pull in, 'After a word from Norwich City captain Matt Jackson, it will be Chris Goreham'. I felt a stomach churn like I was being introduced to The Queen before the cup final.

I had set about trying to learn the Dutch names in the Heerenveen squad in the build-up to the match with a studiousness that had been sadly lacking during my all-too-recent exam revision. If I had paid more attention to those science textbooks I might have learnt something about the dangers of being outside during a thunderstorm. When hail and rain began lashing down, accompanied by angry rumbles of thunder and a distant flash of lightning, the action in the sky quickly became more explosive than anything on the pitch. It was one of those terrific storms that only an afternoon in the height of the British summer can bring, and the referee demonstrated that he had a better sense of perspective about the importance of the match than me. He blew his whistle, halted the game and took the players away down the tunnel.

My first ever commentary subject had, within five minutes, become an empty football pitch with nothing to talk about but the weather.

I gave Roy my best 'help me' look but was met by the glint that was never far away from his eye. Having passed over the mic, he was looking forward to seeing how I was going to handle this, as was Matt Jackson. The City skipper was injured and, as he often did when stricken by a strain, a twist or a pull, had joined us in the commentary box. My best idea was to ask him how his recovery was going. Jackson refused to discuss the subject. 'I've already talked about that,' he said, mischievously, before sliding further back in his seat to enjoy this teenager floundering.

Eventually the players returned to close out their tame 1-1 draw and I squirmed my way through the hiatus and somehow finished my first ever stint of commentary. That baptism of fire, thunderstorms and complicated Dutch names was a good indication of the unpredictability that would follow if I still wanted to talk about Norwich City for a living. Life would never be dull in the commentary box.

It was fitting that such a defining moment for me should be shared with Roy. I had grown up listening to his commentaries on Norwich City's away matches. His descriptive words, passion and humour filled the sizeable gaps left by

Ceefax's jerky pixels and Des Lynam's buzzing *Grandstand* vidiprinter when the Canaries were playing hundreds of miles from home.

I was more than a little star struck by Roy when I first walked into the old BBC Radio Norfolk office in Surrey Street in Norwich as a nervous, awkward teenage work-experience hopeful but would go on to share many of my most memorable Norwich City moments with him.

I drove to Cardiff with Roy and his by-then-permanent match summariser Neil Adams for the 2002 play-off final, sat next to him at Selhurst Park two years later as he described Crystal Palace's 3-0 win over Sunderland – a result which sealed Norwich City's automatic promotion to the Premier League – and 13 months after that we probably broke the record for the fewest words exchanged on a long car journey as we travelled back from covering the 6-0 defeat at Fulham when 'Survival Sunday' became 'Surrender Sunday' and Norwich City's chaotic Snakes And Ladders existence continued to swing from triumph to despair with very little grey in between.

It was that Fulham-inflicted relegation back to the Football League that led to me taking over from Roy as BBC Radio Norfolk's full-time Norwich City commentator. He had spent decades following the club's fortunes up and down the country. At the same time he had presented an iconic afternoon show on the station every weekday, with a three-hour country music show, 'Rodeo Norfolk', thrown in for good measure on Saturday mornings. So, in 2005, BBC Radio Norfolk's biggest name decided that a season in the Premier League was a good way to end the football part of his busy career. Well, partly. Roy continued to cover the Canaries' home matches for another season but I was handed the road atlas, travel sweets and country music compilation CDs that had become the standard on away trips. My confession is that I only maintained two of the three traditions on that list. Let's just say Neil Adams seemed relieved that he was no longer expected to sing along with Daniel O'Donnell on the southbound carriageway of the A11 on a Saturday morning.

I had filled in a handful of times since the Heerenveen debacle and on each occasion the players had stayed on the pitch for the full 90 minutes regardless of the weather conditions, which was a bonus. But the Waller shoes were clown-sized ones to fill and it probably took me a good while to win over a Norfolk audience which, quite rightly, adored Roy and to this day tends to deal with change as keenly as a supermarket cash assistant does when someone tries to pay for the weekly shop in coppers. Yet, regardless of what the poor old audience thought, I loved doing the job straight away.

I was getting paid to watch Norwich City! Talk about landing on my feet. Having been a season ticket holder since the age of eight and coming from a family of several yellow and green generations I would have been going to most of the games anyway. Not that I was about to inform my bosses of that fact. They seemed to be quite happy to count this as 'work'.

It was my Ceefax years that made me appreciate the value of the service I was being entrusted to deliver to a county so passionate about its football that it was prepared to pack out Carrow Road in those lean years which ended with a season in League One. At home, 26,000 fans always watch City, while the away support is around 2,000 for your average league game. It doesn't take a mathematical genius to work out that leaves a large potential audience, desperate for their fix of Norwich knowledge when the Canaries are at Manchester United, Carlisle United or Yeovil Town. And I have commentated at all three of those grounds more than once each in my first decade in this job, which demonstrates the Snakes And Ladders existence the club and commentators have lived by.

In recent years local radio has lost its role as the only place
to follow your team away from home. When Norwich City
returned to the Premier League in 2011, it quickly became
apparent that fans in Broads land were turning to broadband
to watch games live online and becoming part of a vast
virtual crowd with the help of social media. An artificial match
atmosphere was being created in bedrooms everywhere with
the added double-edged sword of being able to tell your fellow
fans exactly why you disagree with their opinions at half-time
without the excruciating awkwardness of then having to sit
alongside them for the next 45 minutes.

There's no point complaining about it or trying to shut
the streaming stable door. The online horse has already
bolted. Whether it's legal or not, many supporters now expect
to be able to find a website based in some far off corner of
the globe which is showing footage of every kick of every
Premier League game and a fair few from the Championship.
So we have had to build on the one thing that keeps an
audience coming back to local radio at times of great need.
Whether it's a snow storm with potential to keep the schools
closed, the threat of coastal flooding or Norwich City being 1-0
down away from home with 20 minutes to go, we understand
the area and the magnitude of what is at stake. This makes for
an interesting balancing act when ticking the impartiality box
demanded by the BBC.

Admittedly there have been times when a last minute goal
has led to my professional BBC mask slipping a little. The
delight or despair of having to call the immediate aftermath
of a match-winner for or against the Canaries has seen my
attempt at thoughtful description give way to what, basically,
just boils down to a man shouting. That might succeed in
conveying the drama or feelings of natural excitement that only
sport can produce but fluent, flowery, descriptive commentary

it is not. Perhaps that's why the rain break in that pre-season friendly is still the closest I've ever come to tasting one of those delicious cakes in the TMS box at Lord's.

Whenever I have wobbled on the tightrope of impartiality I have always found John Motson and Barry Davies to be useful safety nets. During World Cups they would cover England v Germany in a very different way to, say, Japan against Cameroon. Understanding that 99.9 per cent of your audience desperately wants one team to win permits the fan who lurks inside every commentator to start twirling the scarf above his head, metaphorically at least. A Norfolk audience expects the story of a game to be told from a Norwich City point of view. If they tune in to hear that the Canaries are 1-0 down, then the opposition aren't winning anywhere near as much as Norwich are losing. It doesn't mean we have to pretend City are playing well all the time; far from it. I could fill several terrible scrapbooks with tales of long trips home from places like Plymouth after humiliating defeats, and capturing that sense of frustration with unblinking honesty is just as important as punching the air on behalf of the whole of Norfolk whenever City do get a goal.

Ultimately my career, as much as the emotional wellbeing of the Norwich City faithful, is in the hands of the players. I have been a Premier League commentator and I have been a League One commentator without doing anything differently. It just depends how good the Canaries are at any particular time. Suffice to say a perfectly executed commentary on a 0-0 draw with Walsall will provoke much less reaction than some shouting about a Simeon Jackson stoppage time winner against Derby County. A commentator can only rise to whatever occasion the players present.

The scream-fest that followed Jackson's goal against the Rams on Easter Monday 2011 has often been replayed and never gets any less embarrassing for me to hear. In context, it was the difference between Norwich being third or second in the Championship with two games to go and it came with almost the last kick of the game. I have never seen a goal celebrated so wildly at Carrow Road. 'The place is going bananas' as Neil Adams put it at the time. In the cold light of any other day it sounds like two fellas getting a bit too carried away for their own good. We had scored a winning goal against Derby County, not Barcelona.

Neil lasted for two more matches as BBC Radio Norfolk's match summariser after that. To be clear, it wasn't the bananas comment that led to his departure; he chose to move on because the financial benefits of promotion to the Premier League meant there was room for a new academy coach at Norwich City. They wanted Neil to turn his part-time coaching role into a full-time one and he had to choose between the touchline and the commentary box.

Somehow he felt able to walk away from the scintillating conversation we used to share along hundreds of miles of the British motorway network and decided that he quite fancied the idea of wearing a tracksuit with his initials on the chest. And so a tiny snowball was set in motion which, by the time it reached the bottom of the mountain just three years later, would see Neil and me sharing altogether different conversations. I was still the commentator but he was now the manager and instead of pontificating about the big Norwich City questions of the day he needed to find all the answers and very quickly.

The new job was always going to be a challenge for him – and it presented challenges for me, too. A man I considered a friend, and who everybody knew I had worked with for a decade, was now in a position that would inevitably lead to me having to ask him some difficult questions at some point.

In fact, from the start, Neil's time as manager was difficult for me to cover. His appointment was not universally approved, and so I had to reflect that in questions to him, although I knew that his big opportunity was the culmination of years of hard work and not just an overnight whim.

Neil had always been keen to get back quickly after commentaries at Bolton, Cardiff or Exeter on a Saturday night because he always had an early start the next day, coaching some of the Canaries' very young academy players. So, while I used my Sundays to search for sympathy about the hours spent on the road the previous day, Neil was out on the touchline at a training ground somewhere passing on his wisdom to hopeful youngsters.

There was always a burning ambition to become a manager and when he guided Norwich City to a thoroughly impressive FA Youth Cup success in 2013, which included winning both legs of the final against Chelsea, it was a tactical triumph that lit up the corridors of power at Carrow Road.

The board realised this ex-commentator did know what he was talking about on the radio for all those years and when patience eventually ran out with Chris Hughton's relegation battle it was Adams who was handed the unenviable task of keeping the club in the Premier League – with games against Fulham, Liverpool, Manchester United, Chelsea and Arsenal in which to do it. He couldn't. But he did earn a crack at managing the club the following season in the Championship. The faith demonstrated by the board looked well placed with Norwich top of the table at the end of September and easily out performing Fulham and Cardiff who had been relegated with them.

It didn't last. As winter set in the Canaries went into free-fall and dropped to eleventh in the table. The first game of 2015 was an FA Cup exit at the hands of Preston and that was the last straw for Neil. His dream job had lasted nine months and ended with a sharp statement which announced that he had 'agreed to resign'– and I kept up my remarkable record of never being at work when a Norwich City manager loses his job.

For a station like BBC Radio Norfolk it's always a big deal when a manager departs. We become a yellow and green version of rolling news, taking calls from fans, ex-players and journalists alike. It's a well-rehearsed formula because we have had to do it so often over the years. As the station's commentator I should really be around to chip in on these momentous days but I never am.

When Neil agreed to resign I was blissfully unaware and feeding the ducks in the communications blackspot that is the banks of Diss Mere with my son. When Chris Hughton was sacked it was 8pm on a Sunday night and so BBC Radio Norfolk was off the air, having joined its usual regional weekend schedule. When Paul Lambert left I was on holiday… and so it goes on.

The most awkward, and perhaps surprising, one to cover was the departure of Bryan Gunn in the turbulent summer of 2009. Having been relegated to the third tier for the first time in half a century and then starting the season by losing 7-1 at home to Colchester United it probably should not have come as that much of a shock. But Gunn had held on to the job for a midweek League Cup tie at Yeovil which Norwich had won 4-0 thanks to a well taken hat-trick from the marquee summer signing Grant Holt. And so, the following Friday afternoon, I boarded a train at London's Paddington station bound for Exeter. The true extent of what covering League One football would be like – lots of very long train journeys to football outposts – was setting in.

Nothing makes you put your reading book down quicker than a call from the office which starts, 'Hi Chris, Bryan Gunn's just been sacked, can we put you on the air?' I tried to find a quiet part of the train. That's how I ended up trying to give my views on the latest shock news from Carrow Road while pressed up against the luggage racks at one end of the carriage. It was an on-air performance that only lasted to the first tunnel and after that I might as well have been holding a yoghurt pot on a string. Frankly, a football correspondent on a speeding train is about as useful as an ashtray on a motorbike.

That episode came after I'd failed to break the news of Glenn Roeder's dismissal (day off) and Peter Grant's departure (at a West End show). It might be an idea for managers to pay to keep me working in the office at all times.

When you are covering the same team every week you inevitably strike up some sort of working relationship with each manager. When you take into account the interviews we conduct before and after each game, and add on the odd one or two around every new signing, I probably speak to the manager of Norwich City around 100 times a year. That is more often than I talk to quite a lot of my family and friends.

Each manager is different in the way he views the media. Some treat the likes of me with a great deal of suspicion and are under the illusion that we represent a slip cordon in a Test Match just waiting to catch them out. Others realise that talking to the media is all part of the manager's lot in an era of rolling sports new coverage on TV and online.

The one thing that every manager has in common is the requirement to be treated with a great deal of care when we go eyeball to eyeball in the obligatory post-match interview. These are often recorded within 15 minutes or so of the final whistle and after a defeat there is always a sense that one slightly misworded question could detonate the track-suited ticking time-bomb. Granted, it's always fun for the audience when a manager loses it with a reporter. It's impossible to resist shouting 'I'd love it' at the television whenever Kevin Keegan appears on the screen after his infamous outburst during Newcastle's failed Premier League title bid in the mid 1990's.

I have always seen my role as a bridge between manager and fans. In the immediate aftermath of a defeat, supporters will phone BBC Radio Norfolk pointing the finger of blame in all sorts of directions but usually squarely at the manager.

The American talk show host Larry King once brilliantly summed up the art of interviewing by saying 'I never learned anything while I was talking.' It is my job to at least give the manager of a losing side an opportunity to explain his decisions. Fans are more interested in what the manager has to say than what I think, despite my proud, trophy-laden record in Championship Manager computer games. Supporters are intelligent enough to read between the lines of an unconvincing or particularly spiky answer to be able to tell when a manager is feeling the heat. Spelling it out with the full Jeremy Paxman treatment every week would soon wear thin for all concerned. There does come a time when tough questions need to be asked and most managers understand that, especially if they feel they have been treated fairly and with respect in the previous weeks. When Peter Grant spoke to us after a particularly uninspiring 1-0 defeat at QPR one night it was clear from his mannerisms and downbeat language that he wasn't in a good place. I felt justified in pushing him on his future and his answer suggested that he didn't have a lot more to give, despite trying all he could to turn Norwich's fortunes round. Sure enough, within 24 hours, he had resigned.

Every so often a manager does go off like a firework and that can be fun, unless it's directed at you. Glenn Roeder always had that in him, as a Norwich City shareholder found out during a verbal dual at one AGM which livened up significantly when the former West Ham and Newcastle boss pointed out that he had missed his interrogator's spell as England manager.

Roeder was a fascinating person to deal with. His ideas about football in general were always engaging and good fun to listen to, but when talking about his own Norwich City team, Glenn's personality would immediately change and he would put on his game face. He flew off the handle in one interview at Ashton Gate after referee Andy D'Urso had awarded a controversial free-kick that led to a late Bristol City winner. I knew I could be in for something memorable when he beckoned me away from the designated interview area. 'I don't want this lot listening to me,' he said, pointing at some Bristol City stewards and officials.

I didn't need to ask any questions. What followed was a passionate rant about how a poor refereeing decision had ruined his day and his team's chances of getting a point. We played the interview in full on BBC Radio Norfolk and a few months later Roeder was fined £1,000 and given a two-match suspended touchline ban by the FA for his criticism of D'Urso. It can be an expensive business talking to us.

So commentating on Norwich has certainly been a journey, as they say on *The X-Factor*.

Who am I kidding? I've barely ever watched *X-Factor*, *Strictly Come Dancing* or any light-entertainment during the winter. While most of the country watches a TV chef, former England rugby player or Hollyoaks actress attempt the pasodoble, I can be found in my natural Saturday night habitat: a motorway service station.

For Norwich City's away game army of fans, these over-priced, unattractive, clinical stop-off points are like stumbling across an oasis in a desert. The weary traveller can spend pounds gaining pounds thanks to the fast food options designed to make sure you don't just stop for a much-needed wee.

When Whigfield released the disco classic *Saturday Night* in 1993 she failed to include a line about watching greasy fried chicken dribble down the chin of a man in a replica football shirt. This suggests the Danish songstress wasn't a regular on Club Canary bus trips because the Saturday night reality for away supporters is not much to sing about.

Of course, Norwich fans are far from the only ones who treat 'those twin imposters' of away victory and away defeat just the same: by having fries with that. I find service stations on a Saturday fascinating. The selection of scarves, shirts and tracksuits on show underlines how much of the motorway traffic at the weekend is down to football fans and teams criss-crossing the country. Yet I have never seen any trouble. There's an unwritten rule that a service station denotes neutral territory. Tensions and rivalries are put on hold as groups of fans pass time in the coffee queues by trying to identify the badges and colours on the chests of their fellow customers. If Jeff Stelling's computer system ever packs up, he should treat himself to an all-day breakfast by the side of the M6. He'd be able to work out most of the day's results by studying the body language of his co-diners.

A service station is no respecter of status. After hundreds of miles of looking out of the window at nothing but tarmac and central reservations, football teams are just as relieved to stretch their legs as their supporters. The initial flutter of excitement when you find yourself having to queue behind the entire MK Dons first team squad quickly gives way to a heart sinking dread, however, when you calculate how long you will be in line for the shot of caffeine required to complete the last hundred or so miles or your journey.

As well as these fine-dining experiences, the football commentary business comes with a fair amount of 'homework' – and if ever a word to automatically elicits a groan from a person of any age it is that one. There is a responsibility to know your stuff and I will spend a good two or three hours before each game sifting the internet for one little gem about each of the players I could be about to watch. This is driven by the constant nagging fear of being lost for words during a lull in play.

A lot of the aforementioned homework goes to waste. Managers never seem to consider my prep when selecting their team. When Norwich City played Huddersfield in 2014-15 I was looking forward to sharing a nugget of information about Terriers' striker Nahki Wells. Did you know the Bermudan striker started his career with a club called Dandy Town Hornets? Who wouldn't want to see them play? Sadly, Wells was not in the Huddersfield squad for the game and that line in my precious dark-red hardback A4 notebook remained unread. That notebook contains thousands of pieces of such unused trivia, and so the opportunity to finally share my Dandy Town discovery now has proved cathartic.

As well as being studious, a local radio commentator requires the ability to untangle a spaghetti junction of cables in seconds. We always have to install our own broadcasting equipment at grounds and the biggest moment of any Saturday afternoon is when the red and green lights burst into life on our little broadcasting box to indicate that contact with the studio in Norfolk has been made successfully. Then, what follows involves several yards of gaffer tape.

Don't worry, I know this is a yellow and green book and not *Fifty Shades of Grey*, but press boxes are what estate agents would describe as 'cosy'. Over the course of a season you tend to get to know your fellow reporters very well, because you spend a couple of hours pressed up against them every Saturday afternoon. And there is a lot of cramped and awkward manoeuvring when some of us are broadcasting and some others are trying to get to the half-time tea or the full-time toilet. So, as soon as the line to the studio has been established for the afternoon, it's time to mitigate the possibility of any lumbering journalist accidentally kicking the wires out of their sockets. And that's why the gaffer tape comes out.

One evening at Upton Park, having plugged everything in, I realised our cables would have to run under the seat in the row directly in front of us. I stuck it all down with the tape to ensure that whoever ended up sitting there wouldn't be able to inadvertently unplug us when things got exciting on the field. It turned out that seat belonged to ex-West Ham hard man Julian Dicks. I've never been more grateful to whoever invented gaffer tape. The thought of climbing between his big old tree trunk legs while he was mid-flow on another radio station was not one to cherish. I don't imagine he would have been thrilled, either.

Things don't always work so effectively. During one match at Barnsley we were taken off the air by a power cut. To give you an idea of how old-fashioned Oakwell was, the gents was basically just a brick wall. There was no roof; you just nipped round the corner and did what you needed to do. So it shouldn't really have come as a huge surprise that the Barnsley grid struggled to cope as more and more laptops were plugged in. The ISDN box we use for commentaries can run on batteries but I didn't have any spare ones. So Neil Adams and I had to rely on whatever juice was left in the ones already inside the machine – and you don't need bungee-jumping when you've experienced the adrenaline rush of the 'low battery' light flickering with 15 minutes still to go. We made it to the end and the game finished 0-0, but for me it was full of excitement I didn't need.

Vowing never to get caught short like that again (especially at a place with a roofless toilet) I now pack spares of everything in the suitcase we use to cart our equipment from car park to press box. I have developed a very good withering expression to meet the inevitable, 'Blimey, have you come for a fortnight?' I've heard that in almost every regional accent at grounds up and down the country from stewards waiting for the *Live at The Apollo* producers to turn up and finally offer that big break in stand-up comedy.

It's not all gaffer tape, boring homework and al-fresco toilet trips. When seasons reach a crescendo there is no better job than being a commentator. It gives you a front row seat. And, when I broadcast live from a triumphant open top bus around the city centre, it gave me a privileged place to stand. I then introduced a promotion-fresh Paul Lambert on the balcony at City Hall to a delighted crowd packing the street below. That's the closest I will ever get to knowing what it must be like to headline Glastonbury. Okay, introduce the headline act at Glastonbury, but you know what I mean.

Those examples underline why I think I have got the best job in the world. I was never any good at actually playing football. That's not false modesty either. When you fail to trouble the selectors at Sprowston High School you give up your dreams of ever scoring the winner for Norwich City at Carrow Road. But those cruel PE teachers could never stop me talking about football and so I dreamed of describing winners at Carrow Road instead.

It feels like I've cheated my way towards being associated with the club I grew up supporting – or at least chatted my way. The Barclay End could never trust me to do the right thing if I was ever one on one with the opposition goalkeeper but if those fans ever can't make it to a match they know BBC Radio Norfolk will be there for them. We get congratulated when we're covering a winning team and have to filter the flak when things aren't going very well on the pitch. Either way, we get swept along on that irresistible yellow and green wave year after year and it's wonderful.

I am fortunate to be able to enjoy my favourite sport and the team I have always supported from a luscious no-man's land where I am not responsible for any of it but I don't have to pay to watch it. I feel very lucky.

Well, most of the time.

There is that recurring dream about having to fill several minutes of radio time after the players have left the field because of a rain delay.

Norfolk born and bred, **Chris Goreham** is BBC Radio Norfolk's sports editor and commentator. If supporters cannot get to Norwich City games, it is his voice which, via radio or the internet, makes them feel as if they are there.

10

From their lowest point for half a century, Norwich City clambered back up the divisions.

And leading the ascent from the front was a man whose own rise was every bit as remarkable.

The fans helped buy him and the fans adored him. Here **Grant Holt** dips into a treasure trove of memories to take us behind the scenes of an epic era at the club.

IT STARTED WITH A TOOTHACHE

BY GRANT HOLT

Norwich was the best time of my career. The journey the club had was incredible: a brilliant thing to be part of. All the factors that went into it – the ingredients that came together, as Delia might say – created something special. And as well as what we achieved, it was the best time of my career in terms of how I played. I think my all round play was at its best at Norwich.

And, of course, I scored a few goals!

But some of my best memories aren't about me scoring. They're about the group of lads we had there and great moments we shared. For instance, the day in May 2011 when we won promotion to the Premier League by winning at Portsmouth was unforgettable.

QPR were already sure of going up. The other guaranteed promotion spot was between us and Cardiff. They were playing at home to Middlesbrough in the afternoon, live on Sky, and our game at Fratton Park was in the evening. If Cardiff won, as pretty much everyone expected them to, it would put them two points ahead of us by the time we kicked off. So, if we didn't win, we'd go into the last game of the season in third place. We were in a hotel in Hampshire and had a team meeting at midday, and the manager, Paul Lambert, said to us, 'Nobody watch the game. It doesn't matter what Cardiff do. We've just got to concentrate on what we are going to do. So nobody watch their game.'

We all went upstairs. I usually roomed with Adam Drury or Russ Martin, and it was Adam that day. We both looked at each other and said, 'Of course we are going to watch the game!' So we put the TV on, sat down and Leroy Lita scored for Middlesbrough after three minutes. We both jumped up and yelled and you could hear muffled cheering from all the other rooms.

Adam and me went to the door, opened it quietly and both stuck our heads out – and everyone was doing the same. Every door all the way up and down the corridor had a couple of Norwich heads poking out, grinning like mad because of the goal, but worried in case one of the coaches had heard the noise.

We went back in the room and sat down. Middlesbrough's second went in and this time you could hear all the Norwich lads cheering. Nobody could even try to keep it down that time.

We had to put our gear on and go down to get on the bus to go to the ground, and by the time we were all on the bus Cardiff were losing 3-0, and we all knew that if they lost and we won, we'd be up. We could be promoted that night! The bus was very quiet. It wasn't usually, but that day it was. Normally we would laugh and joke – not too much, but we were all mates and there would be banter. But that day the bus was really quiet because the realisation had sunk in. We were all thinking that for the first time, it was in our own hands. Win and we are Premier League.

I was sat at the back. I was the captain and a senior player but I felt like a little boy. What people perhaps don't realise is that a lot of players in that squad understood that the only way they would get into the Premier League would be by achieving promotion. I was one of those, definitely. I'd had my 30th birthday the month before. No Premier League club would buy a 30-year-old striker. The only way I would get there was if I went up with a team, and I knew that chances to win promotion don't come around very often, and so I sat there on the bus and knew this was very likely my only chance. I don't mind people talking about me having been a tyre-fitter, because it's true. You do get a bit fed up with the same old story being trotted out all the time, though, but on that bus to Portsmouth I was thinking about where I'd come from and that now I was in touching distance of the Premier League and all that meant. It would be the chance to have my family come and watch me at places like Anfield. I had two kids and another one due any minute, and I could be going into the Premier League – and with a good team and in good form.

By the time we got to Portsmouth's ground, the Cardiff result was confirmed. They'd lost 3-0. As we pulled up outside the ground, the Norwich fans crowded round the bus, and they were going, 'Come on! This is the day! You can do it.' And I was thinking, 'Yeah, I know! But you're not helping!'

The Portsmouth manager, Steve Cotterill, had been on Sky during the coverage of the Cardiff game saying, 'We can beat Norwich to keep this race alive'. A few years later, when I was at Villa on loan, Paul Lambert told me he'd heard that – so he must have been watching the Cardiff game too! – and he'd thought of using it in his team-talk to us, but when he looked around at us in the dressing room and saw that we were all tense, he didn't know what to say to get us right. That was the first and only time he didn't know what to say to us.

Then, just as we were almost ready to go out, Wes Hoola-han said something daft – the sort of thing he did, nothing too bad, just a joke of some sort – and the manager ripped into him. 'You! You haven't achieved anything yet. Nothing. Get your mind on the game!' It was like a safety valve blowing, and it kind of broke the tension and lifted us. When I was at Villa Paul explained, 'I had to have a go at someone. I decided it was going to be Wes or you and then Wes gave me the excuse.'

On the way out Wes was saying, 'Why has he had a go at me?' and he was angry, which always made him play better.

In the first half, I had a chance. But as I turned to hit the ball, a defender gave me a tug and so I miss-hit the volley. I turned around waiting for the penalty. Nothing. So I thought, 'Oh, is it going to be one of those games?'

Zak Whitbread went really close with two headers. Wes had a shot blocked. It was 0-0 at half-time. One of the things the manager said during the break was, 'Get Foxy [David Fox] on the ball more. And, as any Norwich fan will know, five minutes into the second half, Foxy did what he did best – sent over an absolutely spot-on centre from deep on the right and Simeon Jackson did what he did best – anticipate the cross, get a jump on his defender and dive to head in at the far post.

I was so pleased for Simeon. I knew what he brought to the team, and when he got a lot of goals in the run-in, and the only goal that night at Portsmouth, I couldn't have been happier, seriously. There will be some who won't believe me when I say that I honestly didn't want to get all the goals but that was the way we all felt: it was always about the team. If you look at any interview that year from anyone you will hear that we always talked about the team, the squad – and that was genuine.

But I had to let the team down later that night – because I couldn't go out celebrating with them after we'd won. The boys all went out in Southampton but my wife Fay was expecting our third child and we had an appointment the next day for a scan. I couldn't miss that. So I got a lift back to Norwich with one of the directors. I got 28 voicemails from the team calling me names for missing the drink-up. Russ Martin doesn't drink but he'd said that if we got to the Premier League, he'd get bladdered. So even he was out having a drink, but I was missing.

We had flown down to Portsmouth, so our cars were up at Norwich Airport. The director took me there but all the cars were parked tightly and, because we'd expected to all fly back together, Elliott Ward had blocked me in. Typical defender!

I got a lift back to my house, we had the scan the next morning, and then went to the airport when the team were due to land. What a state the boys were in! Me and Fay were there about 50 minutes because everyone wanted to talk to us but none of them was making any sense. But if any team I've played with ever earned a night's celebration it was those lads. They were a special group.

I very nearly wasn't part of it, though, because when I joined the club at the start of the previous season, I almost called the move off.

I'd had a good season at Shrewsbury but we'd lost in the play-off final to a Gillingham team which included Simeon Jackson. I'd been in the PFA League Two team of the year, been Shrewsbury's player of the year and scored 20 league goals. But the chairman, Roland Wycherley, had said, 'If we don't go up and someone comes in for you with the right price, I'll let you go'.

I must have received 30 calls from clubs and agents. Paul Lambert, who was still at Colchester, tried to sign me but the money wasn't enough for Shrewsbury. Then Norwich came in and offered an amount that Shrewsbury were definitely interested in. They'd bought me for £170,000, which was a Shrewsbury record, and Norwich were willing to pay £400,000, so the move was on if I wanted it.

I had never played Norwich at any level and never been to the city. But I'd played with Sammy Clingan at Forest, and when he joined Norwich I had spoken to him about the set-up. I played with Gary Holt at Forest, too, and he told everyone Norfolk was a great place to live. I knew the football club got big crowds and I'd read that they'd sold all their season tickets despite going down to League One.

So my older brother Steven, his son and me travelled down to Norwich by car for me to meet the manager and chief executive. The fee had been agreed, and there was no problem agreeing my money. Bryan Gunn, the manager, told us that people like Wes, Adam and Gary Doherty were staying – very good Championship players. I was more than happy to join. But the medical was a problem. I'd broken my toe and I'd just had an ankle operation. So instead of it all being sorted and me going home, we had to hang around while people talked about my ankle and toe. On the third day, I was up at the Colney training ground and said to Bryan, 'I can't sit in the Holiday Inn for another three days or hang around the training ground. Shrewsbury have started their pre-season, and I need to be training.'

He said, 'There's still an issue with the ankle. The club are not sure.' I said, 'Look. This has to be my last day in Norwich. I either go back to Shrewsbury and say I failed me medical or you get it done today.'

So I think he spoke to Delia and Michael and they decided to go ahead despite whatever the medical had said. Delia told me later her mum, Etty, had watched the play-off final on TV and wanted Norwich to sign me. Thank you Etty, you are obviously a good judge! And so I was a Norwich player.

We had a decent pre-season, then, boosh, we lose 7-1 at home to Colchester. To this day I feel sorry for Michael Theoklitis, the Aussie goalkeeper who had joined from Melbourne City and whose debut it was. He didn't have the best of games, which I suppose is an understatement, but he hadn't been tested in pre-season and then the disaster sort of gathered its own momentum.

Paul Lambert had got Colchester really up for beating us (of course!) but we actually dominated the first 10 minutes. Then, the first thing Theo had to deal with was an under-hit, lobbed back pass from John Otsemobor. Theo ran out, jumped up, but punched thin air and the ball sailed over him. Kevin Lisbie had a tap-in.

That probably slaughtered the keeper's confidence. And then a few minutes later, he had a soft shot from Lisbie but dived and just parried it out straight to Clive Platt for another soft tap-in. Then the pressure on everyone in the home team – with the crowd and the media and everything – meant that we all got sucked into thinking, 'we need to do something quickly'. So we started going for it but made more mistakes. And suddenly it's half-time and we're 5-0 down. It was the lowest I've been during any match at any stage of my career.

Bryan had a right go, which he was entitled to, but some of the lads were in shock, and although we did a little bit better in the second half, we still conceded two more. Theo probably contributed to five of the goals and he was never going to recover from that. Mind you, I'd love to meet the two fans who charged out of their seats onto the side of the pitch and chucked their season tickets at Bryan Gunn – because what a year they missed.

It was quite a start to my spell at a new club, and although I got a hat-trick in a 4-0 League Cup win at Yeovil three days later, Bryan was sacked. We got a draw at Exeter and then I learned that Paul Lambert was going to be manager when we were on the bus going to Brentford. I got a text message from a mate saying Paul had got the job. I was happy with that, because I knew he had wanted me at Colchester, so I figured he'd want me at Norwich.

Paul watched us at Brentford – we lost – and so his first league game in charge was at home to Wycombe. In the build-up to the game, I learned a lot about the new gaffer, and I think that was the match when he, the other players and perhaps the fans got an idea what I could do.

The Wycombe game was on the Saturday. After we'd trained

on the Friday afternoon I went to see a doctor. I'd been hit on a tooth. I think I'd gone to head the ball and got a bang off someone and the tooth was quite achey so I went to a doc and I got some Ibruprofen.

But it got worse and worse and although I did get some sleep in my hotel (the Holiday Inn next to the ground), I woke up at about 11. It was agony and I'd got no pills left. The side of my mouth was pounding and pounding but the hotel reception weren't allowed to give me pills. I couldn't get to sleep so I left the hotel at two in the morning and drove to a petrol station and got a packet of Anadin Extra, and took loads. I still couldn't get a wink.

I was too polite to ring anyone at that time of the morning, so I waited till about half-seven and rang the physio, Simon Spencer. I caught sight of myself in the mirror and thought I looked like the Elephant Man because the side of my face was so swollen.

I had an abscess. The physio rang the doc, who called me at eight and said he couldn't get me anything until ten, when the Boots near the ground would have something ready. So I went over to Boots and got some more pain-killers and got them down me as quick as I could, but by then the manager knew, of course.

He rang me and said, 'What's going on?' and told me he was in the ground and I should go and see him. I was still in agony. My face was still sticking out and it was still really hurting. So there I was, in a state, and in the manager's office for the first time – and that was when he told me, 'You'll just have to dig in. I need you to play, because I am making you captain'. He said he's seen something in me at Shrewsbury, which was why he'd wanted me at Colchester and now it was why he wanted me to be captain.

I couldn't speak, because of my mouth, but that was how I

learned. So that was it. I played. I captained the side. We won
5-2 and I scored two of the goals. I got the first and the last.
The first, after about 15 minutes, was from a Simon Lappin
free-kick from the left. I made my run, used my strength to
get ahead of a defender, and knocked the ball in. The last
was about 20 minutes from the end, a decent finish from a
Cody McDonald pass. I had a chance to complete my second
Norwich hat-trick before the finish, but the goalkeeper blocked
my shot with his legs.

Still, I think that was the night the fans sort of began to
realise what I might bring to the team. They didn't know the
story about my abscess though. The manager did, and the lads
did, and I believe they appreciated me that night. With all that
had gone on, for me to get a couple of goals – and to play well
in other aspects of the game – convinced the manager and the
other players that I might be an asset.

The new manager was brutally honest with us all. He said,
'Look, you've been relegated. If you don't want to be here, I
don't want you here. But if you are ready to stay and play, we
can go on a journey. I am going to go with the model I did at
Colchester. We will be a group. Nobody will be more important
than anybody else, and we'll achieve things together as a group.'

And what we discovered was that Bryan Gunn had brought
in players who were unbelievable at getting a unity. Everyone
bought into the Norwich way. It helped, I think, that it was a
city in the middle of a rural county stuck out on the side of
England. Once you were there, you were there, and there was
none of this bunking off to somewhere you used to play, or
some other big city or anything like that.

Lambert was brilliant at getting the best out of those players: the very best.

On the Thursday before that Wycombe game he had set
up a session where we had three teams and we played a series

of 30-minute games. Beforehand, Lambert said to us, 'I don't care who you are, where you've been or what you've won. The people who play best in these games will play against Wycombe.'

For the Wycombe game, he dropped eight – men like Gary Doc, Wes, Michael Nelson, Darel Russell. It was a shock to them and to the rest of us. Corey Smith got into the team on the strength of what he did in that practice before Wycombe. He hadn't looked ready before that day, but he did well in that session, and Lambert kept his word – picking the players who had taken that opportunity.

By the end of the season, some of the eight were back in the team – but they had to earn selection. And nobody could ever know he was definitely in the team. You could play well for six games, score goals or whatever, but then he'd drop you for some reason – so we were all always on our toes.

And when he made tactical changes – like playing with five at the back, with three centre-backs and two wing-backs, which he did once – the lads believed in what he was doing.

And it didn't matter who played where. If we were playing a diamond system and attacking, and I went out wide, well, some-one else would go up top and I'd stay left midfield for a few minutes. Or if Russell Martin was galloping up-field from right-back, someone would cover. We just filled in for each other.

And another thing was that all the players – all of them – really pulled for each other. We tried to help each other, to make each other look better. That isn't how it is at some clubs sometimes, but that was how it was at Norwich then.

The diamond system, which we settled on eventually, was definitely to make the best use of Wes, who played just behind the front two. But having Chris Martin alongside me upfront was also important in that system because he could latch onto a ball and get a goal and so defenders had to keep an eye on him as well as me.

I am not sure the Norwich fans always appreciated what Chris was doing. Perhaps it was because the club hadn't paid a big fee for him, and that he was a lad from down the road – that he was not someone called Martinovski from somewhere abroad – or what, but I certainly appreciated the way he could find room and get a shot away and on target. In the League One season he was fantastic. Remember the win at Colchester, when we got revenge for the result on the first day of the season? Chrissy was unplayable that day.

The Colchester pitch was a shocker. We thought the game would be off, but the ref said it was all right, and so Chrissy said, 'I'll show them what the pitch is like when I put my first tackle in.' He was like Paul, determined to make a point. And we were all the same. We wanted to get them back for what had happened at Carrow Road. All week we had been thinking, 'We are going to embarrass you like you embarrassed us.' We knew there would be a few tackles flying about but we wanted to show them that we weren't intimidated by them or worried about their pitch. So when we kicked off Chris hit this lad with a tackle and the two of them slid another 25 yards in the mud.

The first goal came because of the conditions. I absolutely wiped out a lad who had caught me a few moments before, the ball shot away on the mud and Chrissy ploughed after it. Being the strong, determined lad he was, there was no stopping him.

There was no stopping any of us that day. We won 5-0. Chrissy got two, Gary 'the Doc' Doherty got one, Oli Johnson got one and I scored the last in the final moments of the game.

Which brings me to another local derby: in the Championship, against a certain team from Suffolk.

I didn't know until I did it that nobody had scored a hat-trick for Norwich against them in the league, but actually I started terribly that day. My touch was off and then I nearly got myself sent off. I'd been saying to the lads, 'Let's not do anything stupid,' but I could probably have been sent off for an early foul on Jack Colback. The only thing that saved me was that he jumped up and there was a free-for all in which, another of their players, Grant Leadbitter, tried to give me some back. Perhaps the ref didn't want to send two off so early, so he just booked me and Leadbitter.

So I stayed on the field, and got the first goal when I chased a ball and nicked it from Darren O'Dea. They wanted handball, but it was nowhere near me hand. I just pushed it away from him and went. And I knew what I was going to do before I got anywhere near the goal: I opened up and hit the ball in the corner. I had never heard a roar like it at Carrow Road.

They equalised quite quickly, but when I got a chance for our second I knew exactly what I would do again. Two days before the game, we'd been working on team shape and Henri Lansbury – an unbelievable passer of the ball – had played a ball when he saw my run. But I hadn't scored, because I tried to dribble the ball around big John Ruddy, which was a daft thing to try. On the Saturday, against Ipswich, I made the same run and Henri found me with the same pass. I saw the keeper coming and I just smashed it early and it went in through his legs.

Before half-time, I caught Damien Delaney in possession. He fouled me to stop me going through on goal and got sent off, and in the break the gaffer said, 'We will score more goals.'

We did. The next one, in front of the Barclay, came when Wes gave the ball to Chrissy and he jinked between about three defenders before setting the ball up me to hit. There was a mass of bodies, but as the ball bounced up I decided to side-foot it with a bit of accuracy. I hit it as sweet as anything and I was off celebrating straight away because I knew it was in. Then 'Wesley scored another one' to get himself a line in my song!

That win over Ipswich was in the November. It kept us up in the promotion-chasing pack and gave us belief and momentum. David Fox was dictating games. Elliot Ward was dominating at the back. And things grew and grew. By the time we had the return game at Portman Road, four games from the end of the season, we had a serious chance of going up.

By then I had ankle trouble that would eventually need surgery and I was operating at about 70 per cent. I didn't score, but we won 5-1 and the feeling was even better than getting a hat-trick in the first game. Ipswich and their fans had wanted to stop all our promotion talk, but instead of being derailed, our promotion push had gathered pace. It was a brilliant feeling.

From my two seasons with Norwich in the Premier League, I'd single out scoring at Anfield in the first season as the top personal moment – because I was really annoyed that I didn't start!

Paul Lambert had told me, 'Look, it's a different level and it will have to be different players and different systems for different games.' But I hadn't had a minute at Old Trafford three weeks earlier, which really griped me, and now he hadn't picked me at Liverpool. But then, when he sent me on at 1-0 to them, I had a feeling that we could get a goal.

We had talked about getting crosses in early in the Prem. So when Anthony Pilkington got a chance, I knew he would sling the ball in and I was already moving. Pilks's centre was heading for the area between the penalty spot and the 18-yard line but out of the corner of my eye I saw the goalkeeper, Pepe Reina, come off his line. I thought, 'You won't get that!'

Jamie Carragher was behind me and Martin Skrtel was in front of me. Skrtel was watching the ball. I nipped in front of him so now I was in front of both defenders and the goalkeeper was still trying to get there. I knew I just had to win the ball, and get anything on it. As it was, it went in like a rocket.

My uncle Geoff is a big Man U fan so he's not fond of Liverpool. He was in a pub in Carlisle raging because I was on the bench. Apparently he said, 'When Grant gets on he will score, and I am going to take me top off and run around all you Scousers'. He kept his word.

I should think the regulars at that pub were delighted that Liverpool thrashed Norwich at Anfield the following season. I played all 90 minutes this time, but couldn't score – and that sort of sums up the campaign for me. Chris Hughton was manager, and he picked me more often than Paul Lambert did in the Premier League, but the football was a struggle.

I won't slag Chris off at all, because he is one of the nicest men I have met and he gave me a new deal when he took over, but I knew by the end of that second season in the Prem that I had a decision to make. Norwich bought Ricky Van Wolfswinkel in the summer and I did not want to be a bit-part player. I didn't want to be on the bench and be a focus for discontent. I didn't want to be living on past glories at the club. I didn't want to taint what I had at Norwich.

So I went to Wigan, but was on loan at Villa when Norwich turned up at Villa Park in April. By the time I got on as a sub, Norwich were losing and I can tell you that the Villa players were shocked that the away fans gave me a big reception. Then, in December 2014, I was at loan at Huddersfield when they went to Carrow Road and got thumped 5-0 in the Championship and I can't begin to put into words what it felt like to hear Norwich supporters singing my name again.

Norwich fans are special and I am really, really proud they took to me. During my time with the club I learned that there was an amazing story about how Norwich got the money together to pay £400,000 for me. The club had just been relegated to League One and season ticket holders were due a price reduction. One of the directors, Michael Foulger, said that if any fans gave up the rebate, he would match their contribution pound for pound. That money, from the fans and from the director, was what funded my move.

So, as well as thanking Delia's mum, Etty, I need to thank Mr Foulger and the fans for the best times of my career. There were people behind the scenes too, like Val Lemmon who was PA to the manager for 25 years. When I was there, if I needed something, Val would sort it out. Then there were the chefs, physios… so many people who make a football club. We shared something special, and it was good.

The only man to win the club's player of the season award three times, **Grant Holt** led and epitomised a barnstorming charge up the divisions. An irrepressible desire to succeed for and with Norwich was evident in everything he did.

11

Standby for confessions.

Mick Dennis has admissions to make, about a time before he supported Norwich and about behaving badly in press boxes.

There are revelations here too about his City odyssey, which began with an insult and has included visits to the directors' room at Carrow Road.

He also reveals why it did not take him to the Royal Box.

IT WAS ALL JOHN BOND'S FAULT

BY MICK DENNIS

It did not start at all well. My career as a sports journalist, my love affair with Norwich, the relationship with the lady who became my wife – all of it. It did not start well. It began, in fact, with John Bond telling my boss that I was useless. And he was right.

Unlike others in this book, I can't recount that I was a Norwich fan from boyhood. I didn't even visit Norfolk until I was 19. My father was from Hockwold, near Thetford, but his family moved to Hounslow, near Heathrow Airport, seeking work, when he was a boy, and that is where I grew up: Hounslow.

Also unlike other Tales in this book, mine does not involve my father nurturing my love of football. It was more the other way around. I played for my primary school team and he came to watch. As I now understand, he wanted to spend what is called these days 'quality time' with me, and offered to take me to local games. So the first team I supported was Hounslow Town and the first time I went to Wembley was to see them in the FA Amateur Cup final. They had a very dashing player called Hunter Devine, whose day job was an actuary. The things you remember!

Then, when I was 12, a school-friend's parents took him and me to Stamford Bridge and for the next several years I supported Chelsea. I know. Sorry. Really, really sorry. This book is full of revelations, but that one is a shocker I know.

After Grammar School I took a year's journalism course in

Harlow, and then landed a job with what was called Eastern
Counties Newspapers and is now Archant. The first time I set
foot in Norfolk was when I went for the job interview in Rouen
Road, Norwich.

I can't even pretend that 'I picked my team and I fell in
love' when I moved to Nelson's county, though. I was too busy
working or, if I had time off, playing football, to pay more than
a handful of visits each season to Carrow Road.

My training as a reporter started in the Yarmouth office of
the Eastern Daily Press. Then I was moved to Dereham and
next to King's Lynn. They were sending me further and further
west along the A47, but I persuaded the newspaper group's
bosses to let me change direction and work at head office in
Norwich.

An even bigger change of direction came when the position
of Norwich City correspondent for the *Evening News* became
vacant and I convinced them somehow that I would be perfect.
It wasn't the culmination of some grand design, or the response
to an inner calling. I had gone into newspapers because I imagined I'd be running around shouting, 'Hold the front page!' But
I had become marooned on night shifts as a sub-editor on the
EDP, and my social life was so dormant I might as well have
been a monk. The football gig was the first available day job
and so I switched my ambition to the back page.

Keith Skipper, the *EDP*'s chief football writer, took me
to the training ground, then at Trowse, and introduced me to
Bond, the manager, and I was launched into football writing.

On August 16, 1975, newly promoted Norwich kicked off
in the top division and I took my place next to 'Skips' in the
Maine Road press box as he dictated a match report down the
telephone line to fill the front of the broadsheet *Pink Un*. All I
had to do was watch, make notes, attend press conferences after
the game and compose a piece the next day for the Monday's

Evening News. I wasn't very complimentary about Norwich, because Manchester City won 3-0. When my report appeared, Bond telephoned my boss, sports editor Peter Ware, with that assessment of my abilities. 'Useless'.

Things didn't get a lot better as the early season games continued. On alternate Saturdays it was my turn to be the *Pink Un* scribe and it was blinking difficult. I was dictating throughout the game, but the action was a lot quicker than the guy at the other end of the phone-line could type, so I was watching one move and trying to remember the one before it while describing the one before that.

My first away game for the *Pink Un* was a 4-4 draw at Burnley. I kept saying things like, 'Then, in yet another twist ...' When it finished I was as exhausted as if I'd been playing and I had no recollection of the order of events in the match. The next morning, back in Norwich, I had to go into the office to pick up a Pink Un and read my own report to discover what had happened. Apparently there had been lots of twists. It read like a description of a 1960s dance contest.

Dictating copy during the course of a match – or sending it from a laptop as is done now – is 'a running report', or as hacks say, 'doing a runner'. I was so bad at doing a runner that I wanted to do a runner. But I didn't. And by trial and error I began to master my new job – thanks, in no small part, to Bond.

Perhaps in a desperate bid to make me less useless, the flamboyant Norwich manager gave me access to the club's inner sanctums. If I went to see him at the training ground, when the morning session ended he would invite me into the coaches' changing room. Then, while he, assistant manager Kenny Brown and youth team coach John Sainty showered, I would sit in the corner. As they dried themselves and got dressed, I got to know the club's big knobs. I joined in the blokey banter when I could and listened intently to their discussion about football and footballers.

If my daily audience with Bond was later in the day, he'd usher me into his office at Carrow Road and let me overhear his side of phone-calls to scouts and other football insiders. On one occasion, when I said I didn't really have anything to write about, he picked up his phone, dialled another club and made a bid for a player.

For away games, whoever was covering the match for Eastern Counties Newspapers – Skipper, me or both of us – travelled in the team bus and stayed overnight in the team hotel. So I got to know the players well. Tony Powell Christened me 'Poison Pen', but with Duncan Forbes ensuring that none of the 'bants' towards me became too barbed, and Martin Peters making sure that I didn't get too heavily involved in the card-school betting, my callow nervousness gave way to brash confidence and I was able to discuss football with footballers.

Nothing like that is possible now. Access to football folk is controlled and limited. But in that very different world of the Seventies, Bond realised that I was his best link with the supporters. So he wanted me to understand what he was trying to do.

It was a football education. He even let me sit in on team-talks. So, for instance, before a game at Brian Clough's Nottingham Forest, I heard him say the following:

'When Shilts has got the ball, close everyone down except the centre-backs – Kenny Burns and Larry Lloyd – because they can't play. They can kick yer. But they can't pass a ball. Cloughie dun't like Shilts launching it upfield, so, if you've got everyone else marked, he'll give it to one of the two centre-backs. When he does, just back off them two and keep everyone else marked. Stick to everyone else like shit to a blanket. Just let Burns or Lloyd have it. Burnsie will try to bring it forward, but if there's no one to give it to, he'll just wellie it out towards a wing. If

Lloydy has got the ball, he'll just bang it down the middle.'

That afternoon I watched as, time after time, the Forest cen-tre backs resorted to hopeful long punts. Clough did nothing to change things. Norwich won. I wrote a very informed report. And I began to scrutinise every game I watched for tactical patterns and systems.

It was obvious, from my close-up view, that Bond had a very good relationship with Sir Arthur South, the chairman – with respect and affection on both sides – and between them they changed Norwich City for ever by lifting horizons.

For the first 70 years of its existence, the club had never managed to play in the top division. Ron Saunders finally took City into the top tier in 1972, playing a kick-and-chase style based on effort, but the stay lasted only two seasons. That was when Bond arrived – and found a club with, frankly, Second Division facilities and outlook. When I started reporting his work, he was spending much of his time trying to improve things: setting up a proper youth team for the first time, build-ing a relationship with Norfolk schools, insisting on getting the training ground pitches improved and demanding the decrepit old changing hut at Trowse was replaced by a modern building. He dictated, too, that his team played a passing game.

As a player at West Ham he had listened and learned as man-ager Ron Greenwood led a cultural change in football, stressing the value of the arts and skills of the game. Bond shared a changing room with men like Bobby Moore and Malcolm Alli-son, who played with the minds as well as their muscles, and he was among those at the club who, almost daily, held informal discussions about the latest tactical ideas in the 'Café Cassettari' around the corner from the stadium. At Trowse, Bond pro-pounded the Greenwood gospel of 'good', attacking football. It was the genesis of 'the Norwich way'.

Sir Arthur was easily persuaded to borrow the money

Bond's standards required. The chairman told me, 'It is better to be broke in the First Division than have money in the bank in the Second. But don't quote me, in case the bank manager reads your paper.'

Bond also received unstinted backing from his lieutenant, Ken Brown – as I can demonstrate by reporting, now, a scoop I kept secret at the time. After one Carrow Road game, I waited until all the other journos had spoken with Bond and cornered him for a private word. I'd noticed him screaming at striker Viv Busby during the game and asked him what his fury had been about. Bond's anger flared again. 'I've fined Buzzer two weeks wages for not trying.'

Wow! That would possibly be a front-page lead for my paper on the Monday. But on the Sunday, Brown phoned me. I knew he wanted something because he called me 'Mickle'. He is still the only person ever to have decided that was my name, and only when he was trying to be really friendly. 'Mickle, did John tell you about fining Buzzer?'

'Yes Ken'.

'Ah. Well don't put it in the paper, Mickle. I'm going to talk to John in the morning before training and get him to change his mind.'

'Um, right.'

'We need Buzzer. We need him playing and happy and confident. I'll sort it out.'

'Well, if there isn't going to be a fine, I won't write about it.'

'Good lad, Mickle'.

Bond did have a temper on him. Yet he was a thoroughly decent man as well as a gifted coach and manager. And after his initial assessment of my useless capabilities, I remained mostly on his good side. There were only two subsequent rows. When Chinese dictator Chairman Mao died, I joked in print that he was the only left-winger Bond hadn't tried to sign. The manager didn't laugh. When he started selecting his son, Kevin, I put the charge of nepotism to Bond, who exploded with rage. The next day's paper carried his fierce and reasoned defence, though, and he understood what I had done.

I got on amicably with most of the players too, although Ted MacDougall threatened to 'do' me and David Jones spent a morning heckling me.

'Super Mac' had been picked by Scotland but was not impressed by the letter from the Scottish FA, which he showed me. It was obviously a standard pro-forma in which the typed words said only:

'Dear

You have been selected for the international match against Report at '

The missing details had been filled in, hurriedly, in ballpoint pen. After the word 'Dear' it just said, 'MacDougall': merely his surname. The recipient told me, 'I've had enough of all this. I'm going to tell them to stick it. I'm not going to play for them any more.'

Wow again. I not only wrote the 'Mac snubs Scots' story for my paper, I flogged it to the national media too. And that was what upset him. With spectacular naivety, the striker had assumed his response to the letter would remain a Norfolk story. To this day, I don't understand that. Another player told me, 'Ted is going to do you'. No details were provided. This time it was me who called Brown. Again he calmed things down.

Jones was a Welsh international. He and his father were walking his dog one Sunday morning when they happened upon the pitch where I was playing, very badly, for Mulbarton. We had a defensive crisis, and I was doing emergency duty at centre-back, which was Jones's position. The opposition had noticed the very obvious fact that I was eight inches shorter than most centre-backs, and kept slinging in crosses and centres. I kept jumping underneath them.

Jones stayed and watched, transfixed by the comedy and happy to give a running commentary about someone who had, it is true, been a tad uncomplimentary in print about his own defending.

'Use both feet', he shouted.

'I'm trying to.'

'Yeah, but try using one at a time.'

For the most part I wrote favourably about Jones and all of his colleagues. I had, without acknowledging it at that stage, become a fan. Yet an attractive woman reporter, with a backside that looked fabulous in Seventies trouser-suits, berated me one day about something I'd written about one of her favourite players, Mick McGuire. She was a Carrow Road regular. We continued the discussion at the newspaper's social club and have been arguing about Norwich players more or less ever since. One year and two months after the publication of this book we will celebrate our ruby wedding anniversary.

The first house Sarah and I bought together was in Brundall. Not many months later, though, Sarah encouraged me to seek a job in Fleet Street and we sold that Brundall home to a Norwich player, Keith Robson. And that is another indication of how different things were in that era. A house belonging to two local paper reporters tempting a top tier footballer? Not these days. Brown helped facilitate the sale. A couple of months later, I met Robson at a game in London. 'We've made your old house really nice,' he said.

Sarah and I might not have got together if I had not been the Norwich City reporter for the *Evening News*. And going to Norwich matches is one of the things we do together. We took our sons as soon as they were old enough but there was a difficult period – for our support, not our marriage! – when I left the (London) *Evening Standard*, where I'd been an executive, and went back to being a football writer. That meant going to matches on Saturdays, and usually not Norwich matches. We continued to go to all the Norwich games that were not on Saturdays, home and away. Then, when the Premier League started staging more and more games on Sundays, I said to the *Daily Express*, 'I'll go anywhere you like but let me work on the day Norwich are not playing'. Amazingly they agreed. Since then, I doubt if we've missed more than three games a season.

My dual role – as a journalist and as a fan – has not led to the difficulties which Charlie Wyett and Simon Thomas talk about in this book, because I've been far less professional than them and never tried to hide (or even moderate) my affection for the great club from the Fine City.

For instance, when Norwich won the League Cup at Wembley, 30 years before that glorious 2015 encounter with Middlesbrough at the same stadium, I disgraced myself by doing a jig of joy in the press box.

I was working at *The Sun* – in the era when Kelvin MacKenzie was the terrifying editor, plumbing new depths of tabloid newspaper excess. Although I was a long way down the pecking order of the paper's football reporters, I had bored the others about Norwich so much that they made room for me at Wembley for the League Cup showdown with Sunderland. It was the 'old Wembley', and the Press were accommodated in a gallery, slung under the roof and extending almost the entire length of one side. It was along the gangway between two rows of seats that I danced my impromptu jig when Asa Hartford's shot was deflected into the net by Sunderland defender Gordon Chisholm.

Incidentally, during my time at Eastern Counties Newspapers, Skipper had left after a row at work, I'd been promoted to the *Eastern Daily Press* and Bill Walker stepped into the *Evening News* position. Before the League Cup final in 1985, I phoned Bill to see if he would be at the match. Alas, he wouldn't. His wife was pregnant and some time past the due date, so the baby was going to be induced on cup final day. 'But', he said, 'I'm going to name the child after a Norwich goal-scorer'. After ten years covering Norwich, Bill moved to the *Hull Daily Mail*. These days he is 'Director, Knowledge Exchange' at the University of Hull. No, I don't know what that means either. But I assume that somewhere on Humberside is a 30-something called Chisholm Own Goal Walker.

There was a decidedly grim aftermath of Wembley in 1985, though. The final was in March. Two months later Norwich were relegated and then, before May ended, the whole of football was plunged into darkness by events at the European Cup final, between Liverpool and Juventus at the Heysel Stadium in Brussels. I was not senior enough at *The Sun* to be involved in covering the game, and so worked in London that day and travelled home expecting to watch it on TV. By the time I switched on, 39 people, most of them Juventus fans, had died when a concrete wall collapsed as they fled marauding Liverpool supporters.

The next morning, back in *The Sun*'s office just off Fleet Street, the paper's political staff were convinced that English clubs were about to be banned from Europe. I was allotted the task of contacting all the clubs affected. That included Norwich, who were already on their summer break. By then, Ken Brown was manager. I tracked him down and broke the news over the phone. In the context of people dying in Belgium, Norwich missing out was an inconsequential detail. But, for Browny – a lovely, lovely man – it was still a blow.

I've written many much happier Norwich City stories. For

instance, I was in the Carrow Road press box for the *Daily Express* for a Premier League victory over Sunderland under Paul Lambert – and found myself sitting very near Mr Wyett, representing *The Sun*, and Jim van Wijk of the Press Association, who is also a big Norwich fan. As a stirring victory unfolded in front of us, away to our left a familiar chant filled the air.

'We're the Snake Pit, we're the Snake Pit, we're the Snake Pit over here!'

The Barclay responded appropriately, and I suggested that Charlie, Jim and I should jump up and yell, 'We're the press box, we're the press box …' The *Daily Mail*'s Laura Williamson looked at me in utter horror. I assured her I was joking. I hadn't been, though.

The football hack pack tolerate my Norwich affection, even if they treat it as an affliction. For example, Henry Winter, then of the *Daily Telegraph*, was very forebearing at a Champions League semi-final. The night before, I'd been with Sarah, one son, her brother and the Yellow Army at Portsmouth, standing to attention as Simeon Jackson dived to head the goal that carried Norwich into the Premier League after an absence of six years. I danced with unknown blokes in the Fratton Park Gents immediately after the game and still had my beer-stained, tear-marked replica Norwich shirt on as I booked into a hotel near Heathrow Airport late that night. The guy behind the hotel desk looked pained at my appearance, but I just grinned away to myself. I was still grinning when I caught my flight at dawn. I grinned all morning and afternoon in Barcelona. And I was still smiling like a village idiot as I took my place in the press box, preposterously high up in the Camp Nou. Winter watched as I sat down next to him and said, 'Mick, you can talk about Norwich for the next ten minutes, but that is all.' I replied, 'That won't be long enough, Henry.' And although, by any sensible definition, a Champions League semi-final between Barcelona and Real Madrid is a significant occasion, it wasn't a big deal for me that night. I'd seen Simeon score the night before!

Sometimes, I wonder if we all care too much about football. When I was at *The Sun*, under intense pressure to get a sensational story every day about the game, I was often struck by the fact that while I was striving to find back-page scoops, the front page was full of real, and often appalling news. This anomaly between what I was doing and what was of true import was particularly true when my stories were not much cop. The worst, I think, was on a particularly slow day when, despite ringing countless contacts and following dozens of leads, there really wasn't much to write. The best story I had, if you could call it that, was that West Ham striker Paul Goddard had a foot injury. So it was that the next day's *Sun* back page shrieked, 'Goddard toe horror!'

Then there is the silly amount of stress I endure when Norwich are struggling – and the even bigger measure of anxiety I suffer when they doing well.

In the build-up to the May 2015 Wembley match the nervous tension became so bad that I had to give myself a talking to. It was at Leeds on a Tuesday night. It was the fourth game in 11 days and the internal dialogue went like this:

'You know it's only a game. All the really important things in your life are good. Everyone you love is well. This feeling of tightness in the pit of your stomach, and the way your jaw and fists are clenched – stop it. It's not good for you. It's silly. Come on. Get a grip.'

But then Jonny Howson scored and my wife and I went loopy.

So is it mad to be mad about Norwich? Sarah says it is life-enriching, and I have to agree. Of course it's not as important as deep stuff, like families or friends. But it helps strengthens bonds within families and forms friendships. And it is a great, unscripted, continuing drama. Plus, it is a catharsis to sing and shout and care.

On a wider level, football is a vigorous force for good in many ways, despite unimaginable amounts of money sloshing around and the stories of men behaving badly. Playing the world's most popular team game teaches youngsters how to work with others and how to deal with success and failure. And, on a different level, organisations like the Norwich City Community Sport Foundation change lives. One of my greatest joys is that my double life as a journalist and a fan has given me a profile and a knowledge base that the NCCSF think is useful and I am able to serve them as a trustee. They use the substantial power of football and the club's 'brand' to engage people. Some of the results have made me inexpressibly proud to be tangentially involved – homeless folk receiving job-training, 'difficult' children starting to learn at school because of an NCCSF education programme or just kids with disabilities having a laugh.

So supporting Norwich is a good thing. And it is an especially good thing when there is the absolute bliss of beating Ipswich. When the fates decreed that Norwich would face them in the 2015 play-off semi-finals, I gave myself another talking to. 'We're better than them. We're so much better than them. In a one-off game, they could get lucky, but over two legs, class will tell. We are better than them.'

For the second leg, at Carrow Road, Mr and Mrs Dennis received an invitation to join Delia and Michael W J in the directors' box. Oh, thank you! Don't mind if we do.

Our friendship dates back to my spell at the *Evening Standard*. I wrote a regular column and nearly always mentioned Norwich. The publishing business belonging to Smith and Wynn Jones was based in London and I suppose they noticed that there was a corner of the capital's paper that was for ever

Naaaridge. So I received an invitation, with partner, to attend a Carrow Road game as their guests, with lunch in the Gunn Club at their table. Woohoo!

On the morning of the match, a communication from the club dropped through our letterbox in Hertfordshire, informing us that ticket prices would rocket the following season. On the journey, we stopped as usual as soon as we were in Norfolk to buy an *EDP*. The main headline shouted, 'PRICES SHOCK FOR CITY FANS'.

Over lunch, I plucked up courage and suggested to Delia how the news might have been better managed. I feared, as I criticised their fiefdom, that we would never be invited back. But after thinking for a bit, Delia asked, 'Would you be on my creative committee?' I asked who else was on it. She replied, 'Nobody. I've just invented it.' I said Sarah should be on it too, because by then she had moved into PR, won awards and learned skills I certainly did not possess. Later I learned that Delia and Michael liked the fact that Sarah and I were a double act.

And so began a relationship my wife and I truly value. We are not besties with Smith and Wynn Jones, but they have shown us great kindness and generosity over the years – particularly at a time when, for family reasons, we needed sympathetic support. And in return, on the two or three occasions a season when they invite us to join them in the posh seats, we never betray confidences or do anything to make them regret inviting us. We have used our professional talents and knowledge to help the club when possible.

And so we joined Delia and Michael at Carrow Road for the play-off semi-final second leg.

The etiquette of directors' rooms at football matches is quite odd. The unspoken code of required behaviour is that the two 'sides' are unfailingly polite to each other, and that there is no triumphalism in victory nor rancour in defeat. That might seem antiquated, but when you think what things might be like without an oasis of civilised restraint amid all the passion, you understand why it is good to maintain the urbanity. And, in all that enforced politeness, genuine friendships flourish.

So Delia and Michael were disappointed to learn that the list of names supplied by Ipswich did not include David Sheepshanks. He had been a gracious host to them when he was Ipswich chairman and an ally as chairman of the Football League. So Delia and Michael telephoned him to ask whether it was an oversight that the club he had served for so long had not named him for Carrow Road. 'No, they never invite me,' he said. But he explained that he had bought himself a ticket to sit with the away fans. 'Well', said Delia, 'Come and join us in the boardroom before and afterwards'. You see, Norwich City's joint majority share-holders believe in courtesy and in not spurning people just because situations have altered. And I was delighted to see Sheepshanks there – because I gave him a mighty amount of stick once we'd thrashed his boys. We were so, so much better than them. Etiquette? Schmetiquette. Mind the gap.

Delia and Michael invited Sarah and me to join them in the Royal Box at Wembley. But, for the first time in our friendship, we turned them down. We wanted to be with our family for such a moment in the club's history. In all, ten relatives gathered for the obligatory picture with the arch in the background – and sharing the day with so many kinfolk was another reason it was so special.

And, although we weren't in the Royal Box, when we watched it all again on TV, we saw that there was a lovely moment up there in the very, very posh seats. As the players collected their medals, Delia's mum, Etty, leaned forward from her seat behind Delia to give a thumbs-up sign to Alex Neil. Etty

Smith, well into her 90s, had doubted whether she'd be able to cope at the national stadium, but she was persuaded that she'd be OK. Delia wanted her to be there, you see, to share the day.

Family. That IS what it's all about, isn't it? That and football. As Lou Reed wrote and sang, 'It's such a perfect day. I'm glad I spent it with you'. And what a perfect day it was in May 2015.

It was just another point on the up-and-down graph of supporting our club, though. The nature of football is that successes are transient. There is always another game, another season … more stress. I was, indeed, useless when the adventure began for me but I promise to be good at making my grandkids appreciate the escapades too. Then they'll get a perfect day at some stage.

John Bond died in 2012, three months before his 80th birthday. If you want to see a monument to him, watch City playing the Norwich way and striving to be the best they can. He started that. And so the stress-filled, joyous adventure is his fault. It was my privilege to have been his conduit to the fans, and my utter delight to have become one of them.

Mick Dennis began his career in journalism as a trainee reporter in Great Yarmouth. He went on to hold executive positions on two leading newspapers, write about football for five nationals, become a regular broadcaster – and buy home and away Norwich City season tickets.

TALES FROM THE
CITY

VOLUME TWO
WILL BE PUBLISHED IN 2016